GW01164511

The DRINKTIONARY

The
DRINKTIONARY

The definitive dictionary for the discerning drinker

Paul Convery

The Book Guild Ltd

First published in Great Britain in 2017 by
The Book Guild Ltd
9 Priory Business Park
Wistow Road, Kibworth
Leicestershire, LE8 0RX
Freephone: 0800 999 2982
www.bookguild.co.uk
Email: info@bookguild.co.uk
Twitter: @bookguild

Copyright © 2017 Paul Convery

The right of Paul Convery to be identified as the author of this
work has been asserted by him in accordance with the
Copyright, Design and Patents Act 1988.

All rights reserved. No part of this publication may be
reproduced, transmitted, or stored in a retrieval system, in any form or by any means,
without permission in writing from the publisher, nor be otherwise circulated in
any form of binding or cover other than that in which it is published and without
a similar condition being imposed on the subsequent purchaser.

Typeset in Garamond

Printed and bound in Great Britain by CPI Group (UK) Ltd, Croydon, CR0 4YY

ISBN 978 1912083 084

British Library Cataloguing in Publication Data.
A catalogue record for this book is available from the British Library.

For wordaholics anonymous everywhere

CONTENTS

	Introduction	ix
	Tasting Note	xi
1	THIRST COME, THIRST SERVED: Liquor & Lubrication	1
2	ALL HAIL THE ALE: Beer & Brewing	19
3	VICE ON THE VINE: Wine & Winemaking	45
4	WATERS OF LIFE: Spirits & Distilling	81
5	ROLL OUT THE BARREL: Bottles, Butts & Beverageware	103
6	LIQUID ASSETS: Licensed Premises & the Drinks Trade	129
7	OMNES BLOTTO: Drinking & Drunkenness	145
8	ALCOHOLICS SYNONYMOUS: A Treasury of Topers & Tipplers	171
9	ALCOHOLOCAUST: Addiction & Abuse	185
10	UPON SOBER REFLECTION: Temperance & Teetotalism	199
	Select Bibliography & Webliography	207
	An A–Z of Entries	211

INTRODUCTION

Welcome to the *Drinktionary* **– the ultimate lexicon of liquor.**

A first in the field of lexicography and a fount of distilled wisdom, this is the dictionary where the drink does all the talking.

Unique in both conception and presentation, the *Drinktionary* showcases a varied and vintage vocabulary of 2000 often unusual and unfamiliar words assembled across ten thematic areas covering the production, distribution, consumption and appreciation of alcoholic beverages of all kinds.

Wordaholics and boozicians of all ages and tastes – those with a thirst for strange words and strong drink alike – will assuredly find something to imbibe and savour on every page of this intoxicating read and indispensable reference work.

And of course, there's no hangover when you're merely drunk on words!

Thirst things first: our opening chapter considers the language of liquor in general – typologies, properties, qualities; the following three chapters, by way of contrast, examine in depth the jargon of the beer, wine and spirits industries respectively.

In chapter 5 we charge our glasses with a bumper glossary of bottles, barrels and assorted drinkware from antiquity to the present day; while chapter 6 revels in the historical vernacular of the public house and the vocabulary of the licensed trade.

Chapter 7 presents a verbal bacchanalia of boozing and bingeing, sampling the idiom of inebriation in its infinite invention; this is complemented by chapter 8's veritable thesaurus of the thirsty, from hopheads and gintellectuals to wine buffs and skid row bums.

Switching focus, chapter 9 explores the darker terminological terrain of hangovers and other health hazards, cataloguing in particular the lingo of the dipso. Finally, with chapter 10 we are home and 'dry' with the argot of abstention and aversion to the demon drink.

All entries have been carefully selected from the most authoritative unabridged dictionaries and extensive word lists available as well as a wide range of specialist resources and learned monographs in both print and electronic media.

There is no scholarly apparatus – parts of speech, variant spellings, etymologies or phonetics – to burden the text. The entries are defined in the compiler's own words with economy of expression and ease of comprehension foremost in mind. Any errors are his and his alone.

So, settle down, sit back and take a deep, satisfying draught from the *Drinktionary* – the definitive dictionary for the discerning drinker.

Please read responsibly!

Paul Convery, Glasgow, April 2017

TASTING NOTE

The compiler of the *Drinktionary* has perforce made a somewhat subjective call on where to place entries dealing with certain 'anomalous' types of drink.

Although cider should not properly be classified as a beer – it contains no malt or hops – in typical alcoholic strength, in the measures and glassware by which it is traditionally served in bars, and in the style of its modern product marketing, it nonetheless shares much in common with its rival and more widely consumed brew; entries on cider will therefore be found under chapter 2, Beer.

As for mead, although beer-yeast is now often used in the production of this ancient beverage, and though it might conjure colourful images of carousing Norse warriors downing foaming flagons of the stuff in some rough banqueting hall of yore, it is strictly speaking a honey-wine, not a brew, and is considered as such under chapter 3, Wine.

In contrast, saké, though often called a rice-wine, is produced from a grain and essentially brewed in the manner of a beer; however, although it is not distilled either it is perhaps more akin to a traditional spirituous liquor in terms of mouthfeel, quantity consumed at a sitting, tippling etiquette and so forth, and hence references will be found under chapter 4, Spirits.

The compiler craves his readers' indulgence in his choices.

1

THIRST COME, THIRST SERVED

– LIQUOR & LUBRICATION –

A

alcohol * according to the alchemists, 'al-kohl' or the sublimated 'essence' of a substance; according to the chemists, a simple organic compound, colourless, volatile and flammable in liquid form; according to common wisdom, the intoxicating element in fermented or distilled liquors such as beer, wine and spirits – or just plain old booze itself

alcohol absolutum * pure ethanol, free of water or any organic impurities, used as an industrial solvent or engine fuel; strictly not intended for human consumption

alcohol dilutum * diluted alcohol, containing 50% by volume of absolute alcohol and distilled water, close in strength to standard commercial proof spirit

alcohol ethylicum * otherwise known as ethanol, or 'drinking alcohol'

alcohol methylicum * otherwise known as methanol, or wood alcohol

alcoholature * an alcoholic tincture prepared with macerated plant or vegetable material for pharmacological application, rather than recreational consumption

alcoholicity * the quality, particularly the strength, of any given alcoholic beverage

alcoholization * the suffusion or saturation of a food-stuff such as fruit with alcohol

alcoometer * an instrument for measuring the concentration of ethanol in a prepared drink

alcopop * a sweet, often carbonated beverage blending soft soda pop with alcohol

alleviator * a tonic libation, or alcoholic 'pick-me-up'

ante-meridian * a stiff drink to dispel the morning brain-fog and clear a heavy head

anthine * an alcoholic drink or decoction infused with flowers to impart or improve flavour

anti-fogmatic * a tipple taken to counter the effects of dampness or wet weather

antizymotic * an agent which prevents or arrests the process of fermentation

aperitif * a pre-prandial alcoholic beverage, typically flavoured with herbals, acting to stimulate the appetite

appale * of liquor, to go flat or stale

archilaugh * a drink or round bought in return or as a reciprocal social gesture

B

balderdash * any unpalatable mix of incompatible liquors

balductum * posset, being a mulled alcoholic draught mixed with milk

baptized * with regard to wines or spirits, watered down

beliquor * to steep in liquor; to alcoholize

bene-bowse * strong liquor of good quality

beverage * any drink specially prepared for human consumption

biberage * drink given as payment in kind or by way of a reward for some service

Bibesia * Roman goddess of beverages and banqueting; poetically, the Land of Thirst

bibibles * strong drink

bilgewater * thin, tasteless drink; bad booze

boisson-totem * the signature drink of a nation or distinctive social group

bottled lightning * any cheap but strong booze

bottomer * the draught that empties the glass or tankard

broaching * the first liquor drawn from a newly tapped cask

Brummagem wine * any adulterated or mixed alcoholic drink

bumper * a charged glass of alcohol, especially one raised in toast or celebration

buvable * describes a beverage that is eminently drinkable

C

caudle * a sugared and spiced hot alcoholic broth drunk during the middle ages as a medicinal preparation

caulker * a final dram or finishing glass of grog; it puts a 'seal' on the evening's carousing

chasse-café * an alcoholic drink taken after the coffee course to 'chase' the bitter taste away

chemesthesis * in relation to drink, the sensations alcohol variously produces on the taste buds, buccal mucosa, gullet and stomach

chirruper * a bonus glass of alcohol to cheer one's spirits

consolation * alcohol, viewed as a welcome comfort from life's tribulations and woes

copus * a large measure of alcohol imposed as a fine for breach of college etiquette

corpse-reviver * any potent mixed drink, especially a pick-me-up for a hangover

cosmos * a transcription error for koumiss, a lightly intoxicating refreshment fermented from mare's milk and one of the few examples of alcohol obtained from animal, as opposed to vegetable, sources

D

damask * to mull or warm an alcoholic beverage

dealcoholization * the process of removing all or most of the ethanol from a drink

debilitate * to make strong drink weak

degrees Gay-Lussac * an international scale of measurement for Alcohol By Volume, used to determine the ethanol concentration or strength of a beverage expressed as a percentage ABV of the standard 100ml sample

dehorn * a form of denatured ethanol also known as rubbing alcohol or surgical spirit; ingestion is entirely unsafe and is generally not attempted other than by the incurably alcoholic

denatonium benzoate * a highly disagreeable bittering agent used to, inter alia, denature ethyl alcohol to render it unpotable

denaturation * the action of adding toxic chemicals to ethanol to make it so unpleasant as to deter its consumption

deoch-an-doris * the parting glass; one for the proverbial road

digester * an after-dinner alcoholic drink taken as an aid to digestion

dispirited * of strong liquor, rendered flat or stale

distempering * of intoxicating drink, acting to overthrow the senses

ditchwateriness * the quality of blandness or insipidity in a beverage

draught * the physiological process of drinking, whereby fluid is drawn into the mouth and passed down the gullet to the stomach; by extension, a measure of drink

drinkage * the quantity of alcoholic beverage shifted at a sitting

drinkworthy * of sufficient cleanliness or quality to consume as a beverage

drinkypoo * in playful humour, an alcoholic drink

dwale * strong drink; specifically, a draught with stupefying or soporific properties

E

ebrietating * alcoholically potent, so serving to intoxicate

elixir * the essence of a naturally occurring substance held in hydro-alcoholic solution

ethanol * ethyl alcohol, or 'drinking alcohol', the primary alcohol found in most beverages; in moderation it induces a mild euphoria, relieves stress and softens inhibition, but in excess it serves to impair judgement and degrade motor function

ethenol * vinyl alcohol, a non-potable compound; it has been detected in quantity in the molecular gas and dust cloud Sagittarius B2, located close to galactic centre

F

favourite vice * one's proverbial 'poison', or preferred alcoholic drink

fearnought * a drink to boost one's morale or bolster one's bravado

febrifuge * a cooling drink

fermentation * the organic metabolic process whereby yeast converts sugar into carbon dioxide and ethanol by enzymatic action

fermentology * the science of fermentation, especially as applied to the manufacture of alcoholic beverages

fogram * nautical slang for booze of no remarkable quality

fumosity * the heady fumes of alcoholic drink, or the vapours from a drunken belch

G

galactozyme * any drink procured by the fermentation of milk

gargle * a vernacular expression for strong drink

giggle-water * jocularly, any intoxicating liquor

H

heeltap * a drop of liquor left in the glass after drinking

hellbroth * any mixed or magical brew that is as potent as it is unpleasant

hocus * drugged or spiked liquor; colloquially, a 'Mickey Finn'

I

intoxicant * a substance that induces intoxication, such as alcoholic drink

invigorator * an alcoholic draught with stimulating or tonic effect

J

jollop * intoxicating liquor with marked efficacy as an aperient

joy-juice * a felicitous figure of speech for booze

L

lavative * a drink to wash down food or medicine; a chaser of sorts

libament * a drink offering to a deity

libation * a mock-pompous locution for an alcoholic drink

liquid lunch * a midday meal where intoxicating drink rather than food is consumed

liquor * fermented or distilled drink in general; it has specialist meanings in both the lexicon of brewing, where it means the water sourced and used in the production of beer, and in distilling, where it can refer to distilled water used to break down spirits

lotion * colloquially, alcoholic drink

lubrication * alcohol, being the best 'social lubricant' known to humankind

lushings * a great quantity or abundance of strong drink

lymphate * in respect of any alcoholic beverage, watered down

M

malternative * an informal synonym for alcopop

matrimony * Victorian slang for a mixture of two alcoholic drinks

methanol * methyl or 'wood' alcohol; it is potentially fatal if consumed

methylated spirits * denatured alcohol; methanol is a common denaturant for ethanol

methystic * any agent producing alcoholic intoxication

modicum * a modest measure of strong drink, no more than a shot

mouthwash * poor-quality gargle

N

nightcap * a tipple before bedtime

non-alcoholic beverage * any 'soft' as opposed to 'strong' or intoxicating drink

non-beverage alcohol * any manufactured liquid such as mouthwash, surgical spirit or aftershave that contains alcohol but is not intended to be drunk

noonshine * an alcoholic refreshment taken at midday or during the afternoon

nor'-wester * a bracing slug of intoxicating liquor

nux-vomicize * to adulterate proof spirit with nux vomica

P

panther-piss * strong and unpalatable bootleg liquor

phlegm-cutter * an old soak's first stiff drink of the day

pitcher-meat * figuratively, alcoholic drink

pocill * a modest draught or small cupful of liquor

poculent * safe or suitable for drinking

posset * a hot preparation of milk curdled with wine, ale or the like formerly taken medicinally; cardus posset, made with milk thistle, was once a popular remedy for liver ailments

post-meridian * an appetizing alcoholic drink enjoyed some time before dinner

potability * fitness for drinking, the fluid being free from poisons or impurities

potatories * an old generic term for alcoholic drink

potence * the intoxicating element or principle in drink

potiuncle * a little drink

potorious * pertaining to alcoholic drink

prelibation * a nonce-word understood to mean a 'drink before drinking'

propoma * a honeyed aperitif popular in the early modern period

pussyfoot * of drink, not intoxicating; alternatively, a non-alcoholic cocktail

THE DRINKTIONARY

Q

quaffable * easy on the palate, so pleasant enough to drink in fair quantities

quantum * a dash of alcoholic refreshment

quintessence * ethyl alcohol, as first separated by the new process of distillation or rectification of wine, and regarded by the medieval alchemists responsible as a higher principle or 'fifth essence', being a superior form of water or universal solvent

R

rambooze * a generic term for any hot mixed alcoholic concoction, with other ingredients, widely enjoyed in the nineteenth century in the universities

refreshment * a reviving light drink; euphemistically, a draught of alcohol

reposer * a late, last drink; a nightcap

revelation * intoxicating liquor, in that it so often evokes 'an outpouring of the spirit'

River Ouse * rhyming slang for booze

rookus-juice * Prohibition-era vernacular for strong but poor-quality illicit drink

rosiner * a generous pick-me-up or stiffener; rosin, meanwhile, was once a jocular dialectal term for a measure of liquor bought for fiddle players performing at a party

rumbowling * inferior or adulterated drink; weak grog

S

sicer * an early term for intoxicating drink with etymological roots stretching back to Old Testament Hebrew

skinful * a quantity of drink sufficient to intoxicate

sloshery * an old cant term for alcoholic drink

smahan * a snorter or snifter of any intoxicating Irish liquor

smirking * of liquor, sparkling or effervescent

snowbroth * very cold liquor

sorbicle * a preparation that is 'sorbile' – that is, may be drunk or supped

sprightful * of a drink, with alcohol added; impregnated with intoxicating liquor

squencher * a draught to quench or slake one's thirst

stimulants * alcoholic drinks considered collectively

stirrup-cup * a fortifying drink offered to a person on horseback upon either departing or dismounting

strongers * intoxicating drink; also old nautical slang for 'paint stripper'

supernacular * of liquor, first rate

supernaculum * a tipple fit to be drunk to the very last drop

supping-stuff * booze, generically

swish-swash * any weak or watery beverage, or slops

swizzlement * inebriating drink

synthehol * in fantasy fiction, surrogate liquor that does not induce a hangover

T

tears of the tankard * drops of good liquor spilt onto a careless drinker's clothing

tickle-brain * humorously, any overpowering beverage

tiltings * the dregs of liquor remaining in a drained cask

tincture * a measure of some strong drink taken for, ahem, 'medicinal' purposes; more properly, an alcoholic extract of plant material or officinal dissolved in alcohol

tipplage * intoxicating drink in general

trimmings * Victorian-era vernacular for booze masked and furtively consumed

U

ullage * the quantity of bottled or barrelled beverage lost in shipping or storage or short due to under-filling, as measured by the container's air-pocket or 'headspace'

unalcoholized * alcohol-free

uninebriating * of a beverage, failing to intoxicate

V

vinasse * a liquid residue or byproduct of the fermentation or distillation of alcoholic liquor

vinic * in chemistry, obtained or derived from alcohol

vitamin XXX * street slang for alcohol

W

water bewitched * any weak or overly diluted grog

whoopensocker * an American regional expression for an outsize measure of potent drink

Z

zeoscope * an apparatus formerly used to measure the alcoholic content or strength of a liquid through ascertaining its exact boiling point

zumology * a learned treatise on the fermentation of liquors

zymase * a group of enzymes used by yeast to transform sugar into alcohol by the process of fermentation

zymolysis * the action of fermentation, notably the anaerobic breakdown of sugar into alcohol

zymosimetry * measurement of the degree of fermentation a liquor is undergoing

zymotechnology * the scientific study or practical art of fermentation

zymurgy * the branch of chemistry dealing with fermentation as applied to the manufacture of alcoholic beverages, embracing brewing, winemaking and distilling

2

ALL HAIL THE ALE

– BEER & BREWING –

A

adhumulone * one of the three alpha acids that lends hopped beer its signature bitter taste

aeppelwin * Old English 'apple wine', or cider

alappanu * an ancient Babylonian bittersweet beer made from pomegranates

aleboly * a late medieval medicinal broth of ale, spices, sugar and bread-sops

aleconner * a bygone ale taster and tester who assayed the quality and measure of brewed beverages sold in taverns across England

alegar * spoiled or sour ale; beeregar is, similarly, sour beer – aka malt vinegar

allslops * a sarcastic judgement on the once-popular Alsopp's ale

anaconda * 'snakebite' – a mix of strong beer and rough cider or scrumpy

apron-washings * a Victorian-era colloquial expression for weak porter beer

archdeacon * a strong ale formerly enjoyed in Merton College, Oxford

ars cervesaria * a medieval guild of master brewers

artesian * a generic term for Australian beer brewed with water drawn from deep wells

attemperator * a device used in brewing to regulate the temperature of the fermenting beer wort

attenuation * a measure controlling sugar conversion into alcohol during brewing; the more diminished in density the beer wort, the drier and stronger the final beer

B

bappir * an ancient Mesopotamian beer-bread; the earliest brews often resembled sops or gruel and required to be drunk using a straw

barleybree * a strong English ale broth

barm * either the foam or froth that appears on beer as it ferments, or the 'head' that appears when poured as the finished beverage

barmigen * a substance responsible for premature yeast flocculation during brewing

beerage * collectively, the wealthy brewing dynasties that flourished in Victorian Britain

beerocracy * government captured by or serving the commercial interests of Big Brewing

beersicle * ice-cold beer, or beer frozen for consumption as an alcoholic popsicle

beerstone * calcium oxalate; a scale found to coat the inner surface of varied brewing apparatus

Belgian lace * the white foam pattern left in the glass after the beer has been drunk

bierzwang * 'beer coercion'; a former custom in Germany that only locally taxed brews were permitted to be sold within the same jurisdiction

boilermaker * formerly, salted beer; now more commonly a reference to an American beer cocktail with whiskey as the complementary drink

bouza * an acidulated wheat beer favoured by the Pharoahs; whence, ultimately, the word 'booze' – possibly

brachetour * a medieval brewer

braggot * a sweet, malty combination of ale and mead, once known as 'hero brew'

brettanomyces * a wild yeast strain responsible for the 'horsey' character of Belgian lambic-style beers

brewage * the process or product of brewing beer

breweriana * brewing memorabilia and beer collectibles

brewership * a body of professional brewers, or the employment of a brewer

brewhaha * beer, colloquially; also an event where craft beer meets stand-up comedy

brewhouse * a brewery

brewster * historically, a female brewer or ale-wife

brilliancy * limpidity, brightness or sparkle with respect to beer quality

British burgundy * jocularly, regular beer or ale

bromelains * enzymes essential to the process of chillproofing beer

bruthen-lead * an older leaden brewing vat or fermenting vessel

bumclink * weak beer brewed to slake the thirst of harvest labourers

burtonization * in brewing, the process of hardening the water by the addition of gypsum to help bring out the full flavour of the hops in the finished beer

C

calandria * an industrial heating apparatus used in brewing beer

carboy * a large bottle popularly used as a fermentation tank in home-brewing

cask-conditioned * describes unsterilized 'real ale' which is allowed to mature naturally in the cask before being drawn as per tradition by hand-pump

cerevisious * pertaining to beer

cerevisium duplex * a strong nineteenth-century American college ale

cervesarius * an archaic term for a brewer or beer merchant

cervisia * beer; fancifully, from Ceres (Roman goddess of grain crops) + 'vis' (Latin: 'strength'), implying beer as an invigorating beverage of divine origin – alas, untrue

chateau collapse-o * old British slang for ale

chhaang * a low-alcohol barley beer widely consumed across the Himalayas

chicha * the generic name applied to native South American beers and brews; it is taken from a fermented corn liquor drunk by the aboriginal peoples of the Andes

chillproof * to treat finished beer to prevent the appearance of haze when chilled

chlorophenolic * a beer fault term denoting an unpleasant plastic-like aroma

cider-country * an area where cider is the established alcoholic beverage of choice

ciderkin * weakly alcoholic cider traditionally drunk as a refreshment by children

cider-master * an experienced maker or manufacturer of cider

cidery * a brewery where cider is produced

clamberskull * any super-strength ale

THE DRINKTIONARY

clovelike * a tasting note identifying the spicy characterisitic of certain wheat beers

congelation * a method for producing stronger beers by freezing and removing water from the brew

coolship * a flat, open-top fermentation vessel where the beer wort is allowed to cool

cooper * a somewhat incestuous beer coupling, being half stout, half porter

D

damper * a glass of ale or stout following a shot of spirits, drunk as a cooler to the firewater

deculming * in brewing, the removal of malt rootlets during the malting process

degrees Plato * an Original Gravity scale used to predict the alcoholic strength of fermenting beer by measuring the level of dissolved sucrose in the brew

doble-doble * a double-strength ale brewed in Elizabethan times

doppelbock * a highly potent continental lager style identifiable by the distinctive '-ator' agent noun suffix typically appended to the names of brews in that class

dragon's milk * an old slang term for strong ale

drayman * one who delivers beer on behalf of a brewery

dryhopping * the addition of fresh hops to casked beer to intensify the aroma

dubbel * a classification embracing a range of dark, malty Belgian Trappist-style ales

E

ebulum * an ancient Celtic elderberry black ale

estery * a beer fault, indicating an excessively fruity taste

eyebright * a strong London ale from the early seventeenth century

F

faro * an archaic sweet variant style of Belgian lambic beer

Father-Whoresonne * beer or ale; a moniker from the sixteenth century

fecula * any starchy sediment or suspended particles found in beer wort

festbier * any occasional German festival beer or one brewed in celebration of some folkloric event

fobbing * an excess of gas in beer or cider, or of foam when pouring a pint

fourquette * a traditional utensil used in brewing beer

foxing * the turning sour of beer

fox-whelp * a historical English cider, now lost

fretting * a brewing term indicating the occurrence of secondary, inactive fermentation

friabilimeter * a device for measuring the mellowness or brewing value of malt grain

G

gambarius * a medieval brewer, notably from the celebrated Cambray area

Gambrinus * a mythical Flemish king who in legend invented beer; according to one version, he could down 144 pints at a single sitting

gatter * a vernacular term for beer, or for booze more generally

gentilize * to take the sharpness out of a particularly acidic batch of cider

gibberellins * plant compounds used in brewing to accelerate the malting process

giracleur * a grain levelling and stripping machine used in the malting process

gluconobacter * a genus of saccharophilic bacteria notorious as a spoilage hazard in beer

godisgood * a name given early to yeast by English brewers

gueuzier * an enthusiastic brewer of gueuze, a sour, fizzy, strong Belgian beer style

gustator cerevisiae * historically, a beer taster by appointment

gyle * the beer of a single brewing; also, beer wort in the process of fermentation

H

hopine * a beer-like beverage that successfully got round US Prohibition liquor laws

hoppenbier * the first common European name for beer, as a brew distinct from ale

huffcap * a heady ale consumed in Elizabethan England

hukster * historically, a woman who bought ale from a brewster and retailed it on

humming October * strong beer from the new season's hops

humulus lupulus * the 'common hop' vine; its seed cones are a major flavouring agent in many modern beers

hydrometer * a device for measuring the sugar content of beer wort by determining its density, allowing an estimate to be made of the beer's eventual alcoholic strength

I

ingenio * a cider mill or press

inky-pinky * an old Scottish term for the very smallest of small, or weak, beers

J

jerrawicke * a name for any old colonial Australian beer or ale

jingle * ale sweetened with nutmeg and apples

jungbukett * the unpleasant aroma of fresh wort or 'green beer'

K

kilning * in brewing, the stage of heating the germinating grains to help impart the traditional malt colour and flavour to the beer

kimnel * a now-obsolete term for a brewing tub or fermentation vessel

klosterbräu * any continental beer historically brewed on monastery or convent grounds

korma * variously referenced as an inferior Gaulish barley beer, a Hunnish millet beer or an early beer made from wheat and honey; the Proto-Celtic word 'kormi' is nevertheless the true root of 'cervisia'

krausening * 'crowning' – the addition of some fermentitious foamy wort to beer maturing in the keg as a means of carbonation; this method is used by tradition in German brewing as well as to produce the likes of effervescent steam beers

kvass * a light, non-malted East European rye beer

L

labeorphilist * an avid collector of beer bottles

lagale * a portmanteau word for a hybrid top- (ale) and bottom- (lager) fermented brew

lagering * the process of ageing beer in cold storage

lagerphone * an improvised percussion instrument featuring beer bottle caps nailed to a pole

lambic * a traditional sour Belgian ale allowed to spontaneously ferment with airborne yeast and bacteria

lantify * to mingle ale with stale urine to lend it strength

lautermash * wort – the sweet run-off extracted from the mashing process during brewing which contains the sugars that will be fermented by the yeast to produce the final beer

lightstruck * describes a flavour defect in beer exposed to the sun or to harsh artificial light; a synonym for 'skunked'

Lintner * a brewing scale which establishes the number of viable enzymes in the malt

Lovibond * the brewing scale by which malt, wort and beer colour is customarily measured

lunatic broth * affectionately, ale

lupuline * pertaining to beer hops, or resembling a hop cluster

lupulite * the bitter flavouring principle active in beer hops

M

malt-bree * any relatively high-alcohol malt liquor, whether beer, ale, lager or stout

maltings * premises where cereal grain is converted into malt in advance of brewing for beer

malt-surrogate * any substitute for malt used in brewing beer

mash-tub * the vat in which ground malt and hot water are mixed to form beer wort; also, by humorous extension, a brewer

meadophily * the collection and cataloguing of beer bottle labels

mealtgesceot * a payment made in ale to a feudal superior

megasphaera * a genus of anaerobic beer spoilage bacteria producing haze and off-flavours in the brew

mercaptans * a class of chemical compounds responsible for skunkiness in bad beer

merissa * Sudanese toasted sorghum beer

merry-go-down * stingo, or strong ale

microbrewery * a brewhouse producing 15,000 or fewer barrels per annum

montejus * an industrial beer-pump or hop-jack

Morocco * a strong, dark Cumbrian ale

mother-in-law * a mixed beverage of equal parts stout and bitter ale

multum * an opiate extract once used by unscrupulous brewers to economize on the use of malt and hops while still delivering a sensation of intoxication

myrcene * an essential hop cone oil with impact on both the flavour and fragrance of beer

N

nanobrewery * a boutique microbrewery producing commercial beer in ultra-small batches

napper tandy * rhyming slang for shandy, or beer diluted with lemonade

ney-beer * an archaic term for beer wort infused with green hops

Ninkasi * the ancient Sumerian tutelary goddess of beer; the 'Hymn to Ninkasi' of c1800BCE is effectively the world's oldest recipe for brewing beer

nippitatum * absolutely top-notch strong ale

nitrokeg * a modern pasteurized, filtered beer delivery and dispensing method; the opposite of cask-conditioned

Norfolk-nog * a historical English dark ale

O

oast-house * a farm building designed for drying hops ahead of brewing

obesumbacterium * *O. proteus*, a yeast spoilage bacterium betrayed by the tell-tale parsnip-like odour it produces in contaminated beer

ochorboc * an old cant term for beer

oil of barley * jocularly, beer

Oktoberfest * a Bavarian lager variant brewed in the spring for autumn consumption

Old Pharaoh * a strong Yorkshire malt beer in favour during the early modern period

opticity * in brewing, a scale for observable beer wort activity

overdecking * the froth or scum covering on fermenting beer

overhopped * of a beer, exceedingly bitter

P

parti-gyle * a brewing technique whereby the first runnings from the mash are used to brew a premium beer, with the second runnings reserved for a weaker beer

penny-wheep * an old dialectal expression for inferior beer, sold at a penny per bottle

peterman * a strong old Flemish wheat beer style, recently revived in lighter form

pevakh * a weak Etruscan beer made from rye, emmer, wheat and honey

Phrygian grog * a reconstructed Iron Age Anatolian braggot-style ale fermented with barley, grapes and honey

pilsener * a pale-coloured lager beer of moderate strength

Pimlico * a defunct nut-brown extra-strength London ale from which the area in which it was brewed and sold quite possibly takes its name

piriwhit * a late medieval concoction of cheap ale and perry, or pear cider

pirliewink * Scottish small beer, made from the wash several times diluted

pißwasser * a contemptuous contemporary colloquialism for insipid, watery beer

pivophilia * the love of all things beer

pommage * a rare historical synonym for cider

pomperkin * small or weak cider made from the residual apple pulp rather than the expressed juice

pongellorum * a term, possibly of military origin, for the original export India pale ale

powsoddy * an ale posset, or beery broth

prima melior * 'bestest beer', as brewed by several monastic orders in the early middle ages and reserved for the enjoyment of the fathers and their notable guests

pruss * spruce beer, an alcoholic brew zinged with the buds and needles of spruce firs

pseudoperonospora * *P. humuli* or downy mildew, a plant pathogen destructive of beer hops

pug-drink * a thin, watery cider formerly consumed by farm labourers in the field

purling * the historical practice of flavouring and preserving ale with wormwood

purl-royal * a bygone winter drink of hot ale spiked with gin or brandy

Q

quadrupel * any super-strength Belgian Trappist or Abbey beer

queer belch * sour or otherwise off beer

R

Reinheitsgebot * a Bavarian beer purity law dating to 1516 – being the oldest food quality regulation in the world

S

Saccharomyces bayanus * the yeast used in cider fermentation – formerly *S. pomorum*

Saccharomyces cerevisiae * commonly, 'brewer's yeast'; ale or top-fermenting yeast

Saccharomyces pastorianus * lager or bottom-fermenting yeast – formerly *S. carlsbergensis*

scurvygrass-ale * an infused brew of yore taken in winter as a source of vitamin C

shakparo * a traditional West African sorghum brew

shamrock * stout laced with a generous dash of Irish whiskey

shandygaff * beer mixed with either lemonade or gingerade

shenkbeer * a defunct weak beer to be drunk quickly before it turned sour

shot-flagon * a free pot of ale 'on the house'

sixteens * an old, lost Oxford ale

skeachen * a type of historical Scottish ale flavoured with herbs rather than hops

slobber * a former cant term for porter beer

solventy * a beer-tasting note recording an off-flavour of acetone or lacquer thinner

sora * a strong Peruvian maize beer consumed in pre-Conquistador times

sparging * also known as lautering, the process of obtaining sweet beer wort from the brew mash by sprinkling or running hot water through the malted grains

St Arnoldus * patron saint of hop-pickers and brewers

staling * the deterioration in flavour and aroma of beer over-exposed to the air

stingo * a dark strong ale, especially associated with Yorkshire

stuykmanden * a brewing vessel traditionally used in the production of Flemish wheat beer

submarino * a glass of beer into which a tequila shot-glass has been 'depth-bombed'

suds factory * jocularly, a brewery

summer-barmed * said of high-alcohol beer that starts to ferment in warm weather

svagdricka * meaning 'weak drink', a style of Swedish low-alcohol or small ale

swankey * colloquially, a weak tipple, in particular table beer

swatan * the earliest recorded word in the English language for beer

T

taplash * cask washings; by extension any insipid, stale or otherwise inferior beer

tegestologist * a collector of beer coasters

three-heads * an old mix of beer, ale and twoops; a precursor of porter

tiswin * an indigenous Mesoamerican maize beer

tolsester * a duty in kind paid to a feudal lord for the privilege of brewing and selling ale

torrification * in brewing, puffing or popping the ale's cereal grains through rapid roasting

Trappist * a celebrated denominator for any form of ale brewed in the Trappist monasteries of Belgium or Holland

treble X * in colonial America, any extra-strong beer attracting extra duty per barrel

tripel * a very strong, somewhat sweet, golden Belgian Abbey ale

tunhoof * ground ivy, a herb used to flavour and preserve ale before hops were introduced to brewing to perform this function

turbidity * haziness in filtered beer, suggesting the product is defective

twibrowen * twice-brewed

twoops * eighteenth-century twopenny ale

U

undercarbonated * said of a beer lacking effervescence

uni-tank * a brewing vessel used as both a fermenting and conditioning tank

upsy English * a strong London beer of old

Urquell * a term denoting 'original source' pilsener lager, from the brewery of that name in Plzeň, Bohemia

utepils * the first beer of the year enjoyed outdoors – a popular Norwegian tradition

uting * the action of steeping cereal grains in the malting phase of the brewing process

W

wallop * a slang term for English mild beer

wampo * beer-tap slops recycled and served afresh

Weihenstephan * the oldest brewery in the world still operating today, established in 1040 as a monastery brewhouse just outside Munich

whirlpooling * the process of spinning the wort in the kettle after the boil is complete

whistle-belly-vengeance * unwholesome, badly digested beer

wort * a sweet liquid malt mash extract boiled then fermented by yeast to produce beer

wusa * a bread-based, porridge-like beer speculated to have been the manna of the Bible

X

xanthohumol * a beer compound with properties hypothesized to protect human cognitive function

Y

yeast-bitten * describes a disagreeable taste found in ale overly exposed to air while brewing

yeovale * a feast with ale provided as the central customary contribution to festivities

yile-tun * a vat or vessel for fermenting beer

yilling * an old Scots term for brewing, or entertaining with, ale

Z

zentner * 100wt, a superseded measure of crops such as hops for beer production

zuckerpilz * saccharomyces – the fungal genus containing the species of yeast used in brewing

zwaartbier * an archaic Belgian 'black beer' style

zymomonas * *Z. mobilis*, the 'cider sickness' bacillus whose fermentation of sugars ruins the batch

zymoscope * a brewing utensil for measuring the fermenting power of yeast

zymotechnics * the art of fermentation, as for example in the creation of craft beers

zymurgist * a brewer

zythepsary * a brewhouse

zythum * an ancient Egyptian malt beer flavoured with varied herbs and spices

3

VICE ON THE VINE

– WINE & WINEMAKING –

A

absinthites * a bitter medicinal wine infused with wormwood

acerglyn * maple wine, a sack-strength mead made with maple syrup

acetobacter * a bacterium which sours and converts wine to vinegar

acidulation * adding natural grape acids to wine to increase its titratable acidity, so regulating desired tartness of taste and preventing spoilage from microorganisms

aeration * the practice of letting wine 'breathe'

alcovinometer * an instrument for measuring the alcoholic strength of wine

Alicant * a once-popular rough sweet Spanish red wine flavoured with mulberry

almacenista * an owner of a modest sherry solera who sells the product on to larger bodegas; alternatively, a dealer or stockholder in wine

ammoniacal * a wine-tasting note hinting at cheese, suggesting over-ripeness in the grape

ampelideous * pertaining to grapevines or the vine family

ampelography * a descriptive effort or treatise on the classification of grapevines or grape varieties cultivated for winemaking

anthocyanins * the polyphenol pigments in grape skins which lend red wine its colour

anthracnose * a fungal disease of vines causing a grape rot known as 'black spot'

apoplexy * in the vocabulary of viticulture, the 'sudden death' of the vine

appassimento * a technique for drying out grapes before pressing to concentrate aroma and flavour, associated chiefly with classic Valpolicella wines

appellation * a legally protected geographical indicator of where wine grapes are grown

archbishop * a mulled and spiced claret formerly popular with Oxbridge undergraduates

argol * a tartar deposited in the casks of wine that has been over-aged or improperly stored

aristippus * an old Canary Islands wine, long lost to modern palates

assemblage * the blending of base wines to produce a specific blend or cuvée batch

astringent * mouth-puckering; a wine-tasting descriptor indicating bitterness or a dry aftertaste

autolytic * denotes an aroma of 'yeasty' acacia floweriness in a wine

autovinification * a method of extracting maximum colour from red grapes, especially with regard to the production of port wine

B

Bacchus * Roman god of wine and intoxication; used poetically for the beverage itself

bastard * any sweetened Peninsular wine enjoyed in Shakespearian times

bâtonnage * the periodic action of stirring the lees to extract the flavours and other sensory components of a wine as it matures in the barrel post-fermentation

beeswinged * displaying beeswing, a fine scum formed on the surface of aged wine or the sediment sometimes found in port; hence, of a wine, old

bentonite * a type of clay, volcanic in origin, commonly used in winemaking as a clarifying agent

bethphany * the conversion of water into wine by supernatural agency, as alleged at Cana

Bismarck * today better known as Black Velvet, a mixture of champagne and stout; reputedly a favourite tipple of the Iron Chancellor himself

bochetomel * a mead made from caramelized honey and fruits, notably berries

botryosphaeria * a fungal pathogen responsible for vineyard dieback and decline

botrytized * describes a grape affected with 'noble rot' or a wine made from such; *Botrytis cinerea*, the noble rot mold, is used to dehydrate grapes for dessert wines

bouquet * the complex layers of perfume discernable in a wine

bourgeois * indicates a French wine of the second class, below the level of cru

Bromian * pertaining epigrammatically to wine or Bacchus, god of wine

bucellas * a Portuguese golden-white wine much exported in the nineteenth century

C

calcatory * a wine-press

capsicumel * mead infused with chili peppers

caritas * 'charity' – an allotment of wine awarded by an abbot to his monks

caroenum * a Roman speciality boiled cooking wine

casse * the incipient souring of wine as indicated by its cloudiness or haziness

caudalie * a unit for measuring the persistence of a wine's finish in seconds

cellar-physic * an old generic term for wine, hinting at its 'medicinal' properties

cépage * any French wine grape variety or species of vine

Chambertin * a Burgundy red; by certain accounts Napoleon's wine of choice

chambré * describes red wine served at room temperature

champagnish * similar to or tasting somewhat like champagne

chaptalization * the process of adding extra sugar to wine to raise its alcohol content

Chardonnization * a coinage despairing of the commercial challenge from New World wine producers and the anticipated homogenization of consumer tastes

charmat * a wine production method whereby sparklers undergo secondary fermentation in large tanks rather than individual bottles, so reducing costs

chloroanisoles * compounds responsible for producing moldy or musty 'cork taint' in wines

clary * a wine made with herbs, spices and honey, popular in the early modern period for its medicinal and narcotic properties

classico * a term signifying a wine from the historic heartland of the Italian

DOCG demarcated zone that made the type in question famous, most notably Chianti

cochineal * an old vernacular term for red wine

comet-hock * a wine or vintage linked to an auspicious meteorological year

Commanderia * made in Cyprus as early as 800BCE, a strong dessert wine and the world's oldest named wine still in production

complantation * in viticulture, planting different wine grapes in a single soil type

complexity * in wine-tasting, the subtle array of aroma and flavour shifts present to the nose or the palate

conditum paradoxum * a sweet peppery wine popular in Roman and Byzantine cuisine

continentality * in vine-growing, the mean temperature contrast across the seasons, and how this climate profile typically affects fruit maturation and wine quality

corkedness * the condition of a wine tainted in taste due to a faulty cork

crémant * meaning 'creaming' or lively, a descriptor for any French sparkling wine that is not champagne

crianza * a Spanish wine aged for at least two years, including one in an oak barrel

cryoextraction * the pressing of grapes subsequent to their refrigeration on the vine, a technique exploited in the manufacture of ice wine

cryptogamic * a fungal grape disease more commonly known as 'grey rot'

cultivar * any cultivated grape variety, used mainly in South African viticulture

cuvaison * the immersion and maceration of grape solids such as skins while red wine is fermenting in the vat so as to impart colour, aroma and body to the wine

cuvée * bulk wine specially blended for uniformity of quality and marketability

cuvier * a room within a chateau or winery where the wine is fermented

D

daktulosphaira * *D. vitifoliae,* the dreaded phylloxera commercial grapevine pest

decantation * the process of pouring wine from the bottle into a separate vessel to separate the liquor from the sediment prior to its subsequent transfer to the glass

defrutum * a reduction of grape juice used in Rome to sweeten and preserve wine

degrees Brix * a scale for measuring the dissolved sugar content in fermenting wine, thereby determining the quantity of alcohol the finished wine will contain

delestage * a process in modern red wine manufacture also known as devatting or 'rack and return'; essentially a gentler form of cuvaison maceration producing a wine lighter in tannins and richer in esters

disgorgement * the action of removing those wine dregs or lees produced in the course of secondary fermentation

domaine * a vineyard or estate that makes and bottles wines from its own grapes

dosage * in the production of champagne, the addition of a quantity of pure cane sugar in a solution of reserve wine to determine the final type and taste of the fizz

E

effervescence * the frisky, fizzy excess of dissolved carbon dioxide in sparkling wines

empress * to tread or press grapes in winemaking

encépagement * a term denoting the proportion of different grape varieties used in a blended wine

enfant-Jésus * a Burgundy red of fine repute

enfumed * of a wine, fusty, smoky or corked

Est! Est!! Est!!! * a muscatel white from Montefiascone once regarded as a wine of surpassing quality – 'it is (the one)!'

estufagem * the unique process involved in producing Madeira, whereby the wine is oven-heated for three months to help it mellow and release its signature flavours

evaporative perstraction * a technique developed to estimate a wine's ideal alcoholic strength or 'sweet spot'

excoriose * a fungal wine grape canker commonly dubbed 'dead arm'

expansive * describes a wine with a range of flavours and textures noted especially in the finish

exuberant * a tasting note complimenting a young wine on its freshness and liveliness

F

Falernian * the most renowned white wine produced in ancient Rome

fermentologist * an expert in the making and manufacture of wine

finesse * a tasting descriptor, judging a wine to be well-balanced and of high quality

flor * the protective veil of yeast which forms on certain fermenting sherry wines, notably the residue responsible for developing the distinctive taste of classic finos

flosculous * of wine, revealing pronounced floral notes when tasted

fortification * strengthening wine with pure alcohol or very strong grape spirit

foulage * the hallowed tradition of crushing wine grapes by foot to extract the juice

Frankenwine * any wine from the Franconia region of Germany; alternatively, any agro-industrial plonk lacking in natural nutrients but abundant in synthetic chemical additives

frizzle * fizz, or champagne

fumarium * anciently, a special smoke chamber used to enhance a wine's flavour through counterfeiting the normal ageing process of the liquor

fustian * a defunct term for wine; white fustian is champagne, red fustian is port

G

galliack * a French white wine of the early modern era

gallization * the addition of water and sugar to unfermented grape juice, so increasing the quantity of wine ultimately produced by this adulteration

garagiste * an alternative modern small-scale wine producer

geosmin * a compound in wine grapes responsible for producing earthy aromas and flavours

geropiga * an unfermented grape juice mix, typically used to adulterate port wine

gluggable * of wine, good and flavoursome to drink

glutathione * a constituent in grape must responsible for oxidative browning in white wine

governo * a long-established technique to encourage fermentation and stabilization in winemaking

grapelage * the gleaning or harvesting of wine grapes

gyropalette * a machine designed to automatically riddle bottles during the second fermentation phase in the production of sparkling wine, champagne included

H

halbtrocken * 'off-dry' as per the German wine classification system

hanepoot * an early South African sweet white wine made from Muscat of Alexandria grapes

helvine * denoting a wine that is straw-yellow in colour

herbaceous * a wine descriptor, noting the presence of vegetal aromas and flavours

hermitage * a white wine from Valence on the Rhône

hippocras * historically, a mulled digestive wine sugared and spiced with cinnamon

hirculation * an affliction of grapevines wherein they grow no fruit

hockamore * an obsolete term for imported German white wine, whence modern-day 'hock'

horizontal * the comparative tasting of different wines from the same vintage

hydromel * a diluted mead drink

I

incrocio * a 'cross' between wine grape varieties, such as Cabernet Sauvignon

invination * the putative presence of Christ's blood in consecrated wine

irp * the wine of the Pharaonic Egyptian elite

J

joven * a young Spanish wine released the year after it was made

K

kieselguhr * fine particles of sedimentary rock used to filter wine

kill-priest * an old cant term for port wine

krasis * the addition of water to sacramental wine

L

Lacrima Christi * 'Christ's tears' – a family of Neapolitan sweet red wines considered the closest modern equivalent to the wines consumed in ancient Rome

lagar * a large Iberian stone trough for treading grapes in winemaking

lazy ballerina * a type of trellis used to train grapevines

Liebfraumilch * 'virgin's milk' wine, also known historically as 'lac virginis'

liquoroso * a style of Italian fortified wine, sweet and high in alcohol

loll-shraub * a Raj-era Anglo-Indian term for claret or Bordeaux red

London particular * Madeira wine as specially imported by capital wine merchants

lora * the wine of the last squeeze, or from the skin of the grapes

lunel * a sweet, unfortified dessert wine formerly made from the muscat grape

Lyaeus * as an epithet of Bacchus, a poetical evocation of wine as the great 'relaxer'

M

macro-oxygenation * the controlled introduction of oxygen during the final phase of fermentation, preventing the production of unpleasant aromas and tastes in the wine

maderize * of wine, especially Madeira, to become unpleasantly cooked or caramelized through excessive exposure to heat during storage

magnum bonum * the 'great good' – a former cant term for wine

Maitrank * an aromatized German wine traditionally served on the May Day holiday

malmsey * a strong, sweet perfumed wine popular in late medieval England

mandragora * an old medicinal liquor otherwise known as mandrake wine

manipulant * a more artisanal winemaker who produces wine only using grapes from their own vineyard holdings

masculine * describes strong, concentrated, tannic wines

masseria * an Italian wine estate

mavrodaphne * 'black laurel', a dark-red Greek dessert wine

meadery * a winery that produces honey wines, or meads

melicrate * a lighter honey wine

meregoutte * the running of grape juice prior to pressing, or wine made from such juice

meritage * a blend word – merit+heritage – for American blended wine

metheglin * a strong, spiced sack mead, from the old Welsh meaning 'healing liquor'

méthode champenoise * a time-honoured and labour-intensive process whereby champagne bubbles are created by manually riddling each individual bottle at the secondary fermentation stage

microbullage * the action of introducing tiny oxygen bubbles into wine to soften the tannins present

microchâteau * a term denoting an artisanal Bordeaux 'garage' wine

microvinification * an intense winemaking effort normally reserved for either very high-quality or experimental batches

millerandage * a viticultural hazard presented by a wine grape bunch with 'shot berries' of differing sizes and stages of maturity

millésime * the vintage date permitted to appear on qualifying French wine labels

minerality * a descriptive note for the characteristic bouquet or taste possessed by a wine made from grapes grown in rocky, mineral soil

mistelle * a sweet white wine from unfermented grape must fortified with spirit, notably brandy; it is mainly used as a base for making vermouth and other wines

moelleux * a term designating wine that is mellow or medium-sweet to taste

monocépage * a wine made entirely from one specific grape variety

monopole * a champagne of a style exclusive to a particular house, or a wine from a vineyard controlled or owned by a single winery or proprietor

monovarietal * produced from a single grape variety

morat * mead flavoured with mulberries

mountflascon * a white table wine of Latium

mousseux * expressing mousse, the effervescent essence of sparkling wine

moustille * a wine term of art applied to the quality of those light whites best served chilled on hot afternoons

mouthfeel * the textural rather than taste sensation of wine in the mouth

mulsum * a honeyed high-alcohol wine drunk in ancient Rome as an aperitif

muscadoodle * a slang rendering of muscatel – allegedly meaning 'wine with flies in it' (not true)

mutism * the fortification of sweet wines through adding alcohol to the grape must

mycoderma vini * wine yeast; essential in converting the sugars contained in wine grapes into alcohol through fermentation

myrtite * myrtleberry wine, once recommended as an antidote to snakebite

N

négociant * a wholesale wine merchant, blender and shipper

negus * a hot port wine punch fragranced with lemon and nutmeg

nittiness * in relation to wine, the condition of being full of small air bubbles

nouveau * defines a fruity young wine produced for prompt consumption

O

oaking * a process intended to simulate the ageing of wine in an oak barrel or keg

oeil-de-perdrix * a tawny red or rosé wine style; also the light pinkish tinge exhibited by white wines such as Meursault

oenanthic * imparting the characteristic perfume of wine

oenochemistry * the chemistry of wines and winemaking

oenocyanin * a tannin-rich grape extract occasionally added to wine to lend extra body

oenogen * any aromatic fume or exhalation produced by wine

oenology * the scientific study of wines and winemaking

oenomancy * in vino veritas – divination by studying the appearance of wine lees

oenomel * wine mixed with honey

oenophily * a consuming love of wine, whether as soak or connoisseur

oenotourism * the recreational sampling and purchasing of wine at the source of its production

Oenotria * the Greek pre-Roman name for Italy – 'Land of Wine'

oidium * a dehydrating, downy mildew grape disease named after the spore responsible

oinopoetic * inspired by wine, or pertaining to winemaking

oligophorous * of wine, naturally weak or otherwise diluted

oloroso * one of the main styles of fortified Spanish sherry, generally fuller in body than a fino, manzanilla or amontillado

omnes * a Victorian vintner's term for 'all odds and ends' or the leavings of various wines rebottled as one blended beverage

omphacomel * honey wine made with verjuice, an acidic expression of unripe grapes

Opimian * a premium vintage from 121BCE, possibly the greatest wine produced in the classical era; by extension, any wine of a celebrated vintage

opulent * a wine-tasting note indicating a smooth, sensuous texture and richness of flavour

organolepsis * the full sensory appreciation and experience of wine – its colour, perfume, texture and not least taste

oxidative * a positive wine-tasting descriptor denoting constrained exposure to oxidation

P

pampination * the trimming and pruning of grapevines

passerillage * allowing wine grapes to hang on the vine until dehydration begins

passito * a term covering 'raisin wines' made by the appassimento method whereby the grapes are sun-dried to concentrate flavour in the juice prior to vinification

pelure d'oignon * the tawny tinge common to rosé wines and certain aged Jura reds

perlant * describes a wine with little sparkle

Peter-see-me * a sweet white Malaga wine popular in England in the seventeenth century

pétillance * the moderately sparkling quality proper to some wines

petiotization * a method – now illegal – of adulterating wines by adding a solution of sugar and water to the marc from which the grape juice has been separated, before recommencing fermentation

phosphotage * the addition of calcium diphosphate to the grape must, a modification of the ancient 'plastering' process intended to hasten fermentation and make the wine keep

phylloxerated * infested with the phylloxera global vineyard scourge; the aphid devastates grapevines by attacking the roots

pigeage * the practice of stomping on wine grapes in open fermentation tanks

pinard * the daily ration of coarse red wine distributed to French frontline troops during the Great War

piquette * pomace wine; a diluted wine substitute manufactured from grape husks

plinkity-plonk * inexpensive and inferior Australian white wine

polyphorous * of wine, full-bodied

polyvinylpolypyrrolidone * a fining agent used in the production of white wine

pomace * the solid grape residue – skins, stalks, seeds and pulp – remaining after expressing the juice for wine

pontacq * a historical French wine, similar to port, latterly also produced in South Africa

posca * a mixture of vinegar and water drunk by Roman legionaries on active service as a substitute for full-strength wine; also, weak wine diluted with the same

Pramnian * a strong, sweet ancient Greek red wine, mentioned in Homer's Iliad

precocious * describes a wine that matures quickly

prefillossero * a rare modern wine type made from the grapes of vines not prophylactically grafted to phylloxera-resistant American rootstock

premox * a white wine fault caused by premature oxidation

pressourhouse * a building or facility containing a wine-press

primeur * a newly produced and recently released wine, to be drunk new

propriétaire * a French wine estate owner

puckery * a wine-tasting note suggesting a measure of astringency

purple para * any inexpensive and inferior Australian port wine

puttonyos * a scale indicating to consumers the sweetness level of Tokay wine

pyment * acid wine mixed with honey and spices; according to legend, a favourite with King Arthur

pyrazines * aromatic grape compounds which contribute to the herbaceous notes common to white wines

Q

quadrimium * a four-year-old or prestige wine

qualitätswein * a designation assigned to better-quality German and Austrian wines

qually * of wine, containing or throwing sediment hence cloudy or turbid

quinquina * a wine style aromatized with quinine, widely enjoyed as an aperitif

quinta * a Portuguese wine estate

R

racemation * the cultivation and gathering of grape clusters

rancio * a distinctive developed characteristic of old dessert or fortified wines; redolent of nuts, butter or overripe fruit

raspays * an old sweet raspberry wine

récoltant * a wine producer who grows their own grapes and uses them exclusively

remontage * a vinicultural technique which helps release the phenolic properties of the grape into the wine

remuage * the manual process of 'riddling' or turning champagne bottles during the secondary fermentation stage so the sediment settles in the neck

resveratrol * an anticarcinogen found abundantly in the skin of red wine grapes

reticent * in winetasting parlance, indicating the paucity of bouquet in a young wine

retro-olfaction * a tasting technique whereby air is nasally expelled while the wine is being savoured in the mouth to better appreciate the 'finish'

Rhenish * an old term for wine imported from the Rhineland

rhodomel * a classical mead aromatized with rose petals, hips or attar

ripasso * a modern winemaking method pioneered in the Valpolicella region of Italy

roberdavy * a medieval white wine exported from Galicia

rompney * a sweet resinated wine from Greece in vogue in the early modern period

rotofermenter * a horizontal fermentation vessel used in winemaking

rotundone * the terpene molecule that imparts Shiraz wine's distinctive peppery aroma

S

sangaree * to prepare sangria, a spiced wine and water beverage

Saprian * an ancient Greek wine perfumed with violets, roses and hyacinths

scheelization * a method of improving wine through the addition of glycerin to the finished product in order to enhance its sweetness without revival of fermentation

scuddiness * the condition of a wine, particularly sherry, being full of sediment

scuppernong * one of the two major classes of native American grape; it tends to create a pungent 'foxy' tang in wines produced from it

semisecco * denotes an off-dry, medium-sweet sparkling wine

Septembral juice * a literary reference to wine dating from the 1650s

sercial * a white Portuguese grape which lends its name to the driest of Madeira sherry styles

sève * a wine's distinctive bouquet and strength, as appreciated through tasting

shedista * a professional but low-budget artisanal winemaker

sherrified * defines a table wine that has become sherry-like due to oxidation

sherris-sack * historically, a dry, amber export sherry from Andalusia

silex * the soil forming the terroir foundation for many of the great Loire valley wines

Sillery * a clear wine from the Marne used in pre-Revolutionary days to toast royalty

simpkin * champagne in Anglo-Indian idiom

solera * a system for maintaining a consistent stock of mature wine, notably sherry, through fractional blending with younger wines refreshing older vintages in the cask

somalamma * a lost wine thought to have been fermented from milkweed vines by priests in Vedic India, and regarded as a divine beverage

soutirage * the practice of racking wine

soyeux * 'silky', denoting an especially smooth and finely textured wine

spätlese * meaning 'late vintaged', a classification reserved for German and Austrian wines specially produced without undergoing chaptalization

spoofilated * jocularly, a take-down term for wine made by trendy or tricksy modern techniques

spritzer * a carbonated beverage of white wine and soda water

spritzig * a wine-tasting expression highlighting the presence of light 'fizzy' notes

spumante * a sweet 'foaming' sparkler

St Vincent Saragossa * patron saint of wine, vintners and vineyards

stalkiness * the heavily tannic or harshly unripe quality of wine produced in too great contact with grape stalks and pips during the pressing of the juice

stepony * a raisin wine widely consumed during the seventeenth century

stravecchio * describes any old and mellow Italian wine, especially Marsala

stumming * the process of reviving fermentation in a vapid wine through the addition of grape must

sulphurated * impregnated with sulfites to prevent the wine oxidizing and spoiling

Super-Tuscans * a loose category of highly priced and smartly marketed cult wines produced in northern Italy

Surrentine * a celebrated ancient Roman vintage from the Sorrento region

süssreserve * unfermented grape must added to wine as a sweetener

Syracuse * a rich red wine produced from the muscat grape

T

tafelwein * ordinary or table wine

tartrates * crystalline deposits which commonly precipitate out of wine over time

teinturier * denotes grapes which are naturally 'dyed' red in the flesh; most red wine grapes produce clear juice which requires to be soaked in the skins to impart colour

terroir * the 'je ne sais quoi' of French viniculture, evoking the soul of the grape and the soil it springs from

thermovinification * a winemaking process involving heating the grapes or must to boiling point prior to fermentation

tirage * the first bottling step in the process of turning a new wine into fizz

Tirosh * in the Bible, grape must or fresh, new wine

torcula * a wine-press

transparency * the ability of a wine to display the full panoply of fruit, floral and mineral notes

transversage * a variant method of making sparkling wine, whereby the wine is disgorged after riddling, transferred to a tank for filtering and then rebottled to preserve its mousse

tribromoanisole * a causative chemical factor in the manifestation of cork taint in wine

trockenbeerenauslese * a dessert wine classification indicating the late harvest of selected dry botrytized berries – such wines are rich in flavour, rare and relatively expensive

typicity * a term denoting how faithfully a wine expresses its varietal origins and provenance

U

unctuous * a wine descriptor meaning variously lush, rich, velvety and intense

uncuted * of wine, dry, brut or sec – that is, not converted into sweet wine

uviferous * bearing vines or grapes

V

vappa * wine gone sour or flat

varietal * a wine made primarily from a single variety of grape

vegetal * in winespeak, more leafy than properly fruity or floral, suggesting a wine made from unripe grapes

vendonging * the grape harvest, or vintage

veraison * in viticulture, the onset of ripening with regard to grape berries or clusters

vermouth * 'wormwood wine', a style of fortified, aromatized white wine

vertical * the comparative tasting of different vintages of the same wine

vigneron * one who cultivates a vineyard for the purposes of winemaking

vignette * a micro-vineyard, typically part of a larger consolidated estate

vin d'honneur * a wine offered to esteemed guests on official or ceremonial occasions; also the title of said reception

vinaceous * of the colour of red wine

vinacre * vinegar, or sour wine

vinarious * pertaining to wine

vindemiatory * pertaining to the vintage, being the gathering of wine grapes

vindemiatrix * a lady vintager

vinegarist * a vinegar manufacturer

vine-garth * a vineyard, or plantation of vines used in the production of wine

vine-husbandry * the action of tending to grapevines

vineyardist * a vine-master, or wine-grower

viniculture * the practical science of growing vines and harvesting grapes exclusively for the production of wine

viniferous * producing wine

vinification * winemaking; the process of fermenting grape juice into alcohol

vinimatic * an enclosed wine fermentation tank with rotating blades

vinitorian * tending to grapevines or pertaining to winemaking

vino maestro * a wine used in blending, notably for topping up lesser wines

vinometry * measurement of the purity or alcoholic content of wine

vinosity * the essential quality of wine; its characteristic texture, taste and tint

vintage * the grape harvest, particularly in regard to a year producing notable wines

vintager * a grape-picker

vinum absinthiatum * wormwood wine, or vermouth

vinum album * white wine

vinum campanum * champagne

vinum portense * port

vinum rubrum * red wine

vinum theologium * premium monastery wine reserved for consumption during the Mass

vinum xericum * sherry

virgin wine * grape juice

viticetum * a vineyard

viticide * any pest or blight that destroys grapevines

viticulturalist * a wine-grower

viticulture * the cultivation of grapevines used in winemaking

vitigineous * coming from the vine

Vitis labrusca * a native New World vine resistant to the depradations of *Phylloxera vastatrix*

Vitis vinifera * the common Eurasian grape; its undomesticated sub-species *V. vinifera sylvestris* is the original source of 99 per cent of the world's wine today

volatile * describes a faulty wine smelling of vinegar

W

warnage * an old sweet Italian wine, anglicized from vernaccia

waterberry * a disorder of vine nutrition also known as bunchstem necrosis, causing ripening wine grapes to shrivel and die, individually or in entire clusters

whippincrust * a wine known to sixteenth century palates, but not today

whitewash * a glass of sherry as a finish, taken after port or claret or after a meal

wineberg * a vineyard

wineland * a grape-belt or winemaking district

winemanship * deep knowledge and discernment in the appreciation of fine wine

winery * a wine-producing facility or business engaged in the wine trade

wine-snobbery * affectation to erudition or sophistication in matters oenological

winespeak * the learned, and sometimes pompous, lexicon of wine

wingemang * an Old English term for a beverage made or mixed with wine

wintrog * a medieval wine-press

X

Ximenes * a sherry or sweet raisin wine from Andalusia

Y

ysell * medieval sour wine resembling vinegar

Z

zarab * a general term for wine, dating from the fifteenth century

zasmidium * *Z. cellare*, a wine cellar mold which thrives on alcohol vapour

zinfandel * a Californian red grape variety and wine, also known as primitivo

4

WATERS OF LIFE

– SPIRITS & DISTILLING –

A

absinthiana * memorabilia or paraphernalia attaching to the rituals of drinking absinthe, a popular bohemian beverage with alleged hallucinogenic properties

acratism * a cordial or similar stiff drink taken before meals as an appetizer

adipson * a strong beverage to allay a strong thirst

alabazam * an old-school cocktail featuring a large dose of Angostura bitters

alcoholizate * to distil a drink by concentrating its spirit, or to undergo distillation

alkermes * a traditional Italian cordial or liqueur whose striking crimson colour is imparted by the crushed kermes insect bodies added to the spice-infused spirit base

angels' share * that portion of whisky lost to evaporation during maturation in the barrel

applejack * 'cider royal' – brandy distilled from cider rather than, more traditionally, wine; popular in colonial America, when cider was 'jacked' or strengthened by freeze-distillation

aqua composita * 'compound water' distilled from strong proof liquor, formerly used to prepare medicinal waters and alcoholic cordials

aqua mirabilis * a 'miracle water' cordial composed of aromatic spices soaked in spirit of wine before being redistilled

aquavit * a popular Scandinavian flavoured spirit distilled from grain or potatoes, traditionally drunk straight and chilled

aqua-vitae * 'water of life' – a generic term for distilled liquor, one reflecting its earliest origins as a therapeutic tonic or tincture

ardaunt * hard liquor, being an 'ardent' or fiery spirit such as brandy

Argentarium * a liqueur produced to this day in a monastery north of Rome, based on brandy flavoured with herbs

Athole brose * a sweet Scottish liqueur-like drink based on strained oatmeal broth liberally laced with whisky; it was said to have been enjoyed by Queen Victoria

atom-bombo * cheap and potent grape spirit, methylated spirits, or a combo thereof

Aurum potabile * 'drinkable gold', a cordial featuring brandy coloured with saffron

awerdenty * firewater; a rough Englishing of 'aguardiente' – high-proof spirit often illicitly produced

B

Badminton cup * a summer cocktail or 'cooler' featuring either gin or curaçao with claret, sugar, soda-water and ice

baijiu * Chinese 'white alcohol', a highly potent 'sorghum wine' reckoned to be the most heavily consumed distilled drink in the world today

barefooted * undiluted in regard to whisky

bimbo * a punch based on cognac, popular in the late nineteenth century

bingo * any hard liquor, but especially brandy

blouperd * 'horse-rider', South African methylated spirits as drunk by the desperate

bluestone * the lowest-quality bathtub gin

botanicals * the diverse fruits, herbs, flowers, roots, barks, seeds or spices variously used to flavour spirits, most notably gin

bourbonization * the introduction of American whiskey-making techniques and flavour profiles into the Scotch whisky industry; the perceived scourge of 'Scourbon'

brandy galaxy * a long-lost American cocktail composed chiefly of brandy and milk

brouillis * the product of the first distillation in the production of cognac

bumbo * an old American toddy or rum cocktail with sugar and nutmeg; reputedly the origin of the term 'bum' denoting an alcoholic derelict

bush champagne * Australian meths, made potable by the addition of river water and smelling salts

C

calibogus * an American colonial-era concoction of rum, spruce beer and molasses

Charenton omnibus * absinthe; Charenton formerly served Paris as a lunatic asylum

clear-crystal * any white spirit, though a term originally reserved for gin

cobbler * an older type of mixed drink typically consisting of a base spirit sweetened with sugar and with fresh fruit and foliage added for decoration

cocktail * traditionally, a spirit-based blended beverage with sugar or syrup and bitters

cohobation * redistillation; an obsolete term from when the science of distilling was yet in its infancy

connywobble * a drink of eggs and brandy whisked together

constitutional * Australian gin and bitters

cool-nantz * French brandy, especially as prized from Nantes

cordial * originally an apothecary's tincture especially intended to invigorate the heart, thereafter evolving into the forerunner of the liqueur as a recreational spirituous intoxicant

cordialine * of the nature of a cordial

cordialize * to prepare or ply with a cordial drink

corporation cocktail * a bleakly humorous expression for coal gas bubbled through milk – a desperate if occasional recourse of Scottish alcoholics in the postwar years; also known as 'electric soup'

cosmopolitan * a vodka-based cocktail, popularized by the TV series *Sex and the City*

cratur * 'the creature', being Irish whiskey

crusta * a style descriptor for any elaborate North American cocktail

D

demoiselle * a tot of Normandy applejack, better known as Calvados

dephlegmator * a reflux condenser, that piece of the distilling apparatus where the alcoholic vapour is allowed to cool

diapente * hot alcoholic punch, containing five ingredients as per tradition

distillage * the process or product of distilling alcohol

distillation * the process of first heating a fermented liquid to allow the lighter volatile elements such as alcohol to evaporate and separate from the water, and then cooling and condensing that vapour back into liquid form as spirit

distillatory * pertaining to distilling; also, a collection of recipes for distilling

distilleress * historically, a woman with expertise in making spirituous liquor

distillery * a building or business where spirituous liquors are produced

distilment * any distilled liquor

E

eau-de-vie * brandy, being the Gallic 'water of life' to the Gaelic 'usquebaugh'

F

family-disturbance * a sardonic term for whisky as a wrecker of domestic harmony

farintosh * an old general term for Scotch whisky

firewater * harsh whisky

fix bayonets * an Anzac name for methylated spirits in orange juice, instilling courage on the battlefields of the Great War

floradora * a classic dry gin cocktail ideally taken as a 'long' drink or cooler

foreshots * the first drops of spirit to come out of the still

French 75 * named after a piece of field ordnance, an explosive cocktail of gin or cognac with champagne, lemon juice and sugar

G

glögg * a Scandinavian winter beverage of spiced and mulled red wine with brandy

grog * originally, rum cut with water; now a term often used for any alcoholic drink

gusano * the worm found floating in a bottle of mezcal liquor – legend has it the drinker will experience psychoactive intoxication if the worm too is consumed; purely a marketing gimmick

H

hailstorm * a style of cocktail made with abundant crushed ice

heartsease * any distilled alcoholic drink, though most notably gin

hokonui * Maori moonshine

hoochinoo * a still for the manufacture of Alaskan bootleg liquor

howling Modoc * an old Western brew of 'bad rum', tobacco and cayenne pepper

humpty-dumpty * brandy with the addition of boiled ale

I

ipsydinxy * a vernacular term from the 1800s for American whiskey

J

Jagerette * a young female recruited to promote Jagermeister, a German digestive shot-drink

jiggerstuff * unlawfully distilled spirits, a jigger being an illicit still

John Barleycorn * the personification of malt liquor or the grain from which it is made

K

kerotakis * an early distillation apparatus used by the Egyptian alchemists

kill-devil * a former name for rum; 'kill-me-quick' was gin

kurabito * a brewer of saké, or rice liquor

L

lembic * a primitive colonial backyard still

liqueur * any strong, sweet spirituous beverage aromatized with fruits, herbs, spices and the like; ideal as an after-dinner drink or added as a cocktail ingredient

liquorist * one skilled in creating new liqueurs, cordials or cocktails

locomotive * a mulled concoction of curacao, burgundy, egg yolks, honey and cloves

louching * the cloudy appearance obtained when water is added to anise-based liqueurs and spirits – otherwise known as the 'ouzo effect'

loveage * tap slops mixed with the leavings of spirit bottles, as sold cheaply in Victorian gin-parlours

M

maceration * the process of infusing spirits with crushed fruits to impart flavour

Madame Geneva * genever or gin, known infamously in eighteenth-century England as 'mother's ruin'

mahogany * a dark Cornish beverage of two parts gin to one part treacle

marc * high-strength brandy distilled from fermented grape-cake

mezcal * the generic name for all spirits distilled from the fermented sap of the agave plant, including tequila

microdistillery * a modern boutique small-production stillhouse

mocktail * any non-alcoholic cocktail

molecular mixology * the principles of molecular chemistry as applied to the preparation of artisanal cocktails

monongahela * American rye whisky

moonshiner * a producer of clandestinely distilled high-proof spirits

mumbo-jum * an archaic style of West Indies punch made with rum

muzzler * a dram-shot of spirits

N

nihonshu * saké, properly; in Japan saké can mean alcoholic beverage generally

nitro-muddling * the use of liquid nitrogen as a quick way of aromatizing cocktails

O

ogogoro * Nigerian gin home-distilled from palm wine

overproof * containing a greater proportion of alcohol than normal proof spirit, especially 50%+ ABV; also the name given to some formidable Navy-strength rums

P

pariah-arrack * an old South Asian spirit typically distilled from coconut palm wine, mixed with cannabis sativa or datura to intensify the experience of intoxication

patent-digester * brandy, as an aid to the digestion of one's meal

paxarette * a sherry concentrate used to season whisky casks, thereby enhancing and enriching the flavour of the spirit

peat-reek * home-distilled Highland whisky, suffused with the aroma of peat smoke from the hearth

penitentiary highball * illicitly distilled prison hooch

persicot * a popular Renaissance liqueur flavoured with macerated peach kernels

philharmonic * rhyming slang for gin and tonic

pisco * unaged Peruvian white brandy

popskull * a Prohibition-years term denoting raw, powerful bootleg whiskey

poteen * small-batch Irish moonshine whiskey

pousse-café * any skilfully 'layered' cocktail such as a tricolour

poverty * gin; what it is wont to reduce the addict to

primitive * in regard to spirits, unmixed or undiluted; 'neat'

puggle-pawnee * 'crazy water', an affectionate Anglo-Indian reference to rum

punchery * any premises where punch – a mixed beverage of alcoholic, usually spirituous, and non-alcoholic ingredients – is prepared

punchifier * one who creates or concocts punch liquors

Q

quare stuff (the) * illicitly distilled Irish whiskey

quartern o'finger * a generous measure of rum

queer-nantz * rank-bad brandy

R

ratafia * a forerunner beverage of the modern liqueur, often domestically produced to a high alcoholic strength, and made by steeping fruits or nuts in a sweet spirit base; it was drunk to conclude or 'ratify' the likes of legal and commercial contracts

rectification * the process of purifying ethanol by means of repeated distillation; rectified or 'neutral' spirit is used inter alia in blending whisky and as a mixing agent in the preparation of punches, cocktails and liqueurs

reverent * an American regionalism denoting a superior-quality whiskey or brandy

rosasolis * a once-popular sweet aphrodisiacal cordial made from juice of sundew

rotovap * a piece of low-pressure vacuum distillation equipment

Royal Usquebaugh * an early spiced liqueur fortified with specks of gold leaf

rumbullion * strong distilled liquor

rumbustion * trisyllabic rum

rumfustian * a hot drink of gin and various spices, once popular as a nightcap

rummager * a mechanism for stirring the liquor in coal-fired pot-stills

rummery * a rum distillery

S

sagwire * distilled Malay palm wine, dubbed 'hell water' by the early Dutch colonists on account of its potency and pungency

sakery * a saké manufactory; the authentic Japanese term is 'sakagura'

sallivocus * a Scottish punch comprising spirits and wine in equal proportion

samogon * home-distilled Russian vodka

sampson * a warmed combination of rum and hard cider

samshoo * any fiery Chinese liquor distilled from rice or sorghum

scotchem * applejack in boiling water with a dash of powdered mustard, formerly served in taverns across colonial-era America to invigorate cold and weary travellers

Scotchification * a term in reproach of the perceived trend within the American bourbon and wider premium liquor market for producers to emulate Scotch whisky styles, launching new brands that are deemed too-long aged and overly expensive

serpentary * an early retort or still

silver-fizz * a nineteenth-century gin-based effervescent cocktail

Simon pure * said of whisky considered to be of the highest quality

singlings * in making moonshine whisky, the first batch of crude distillation thereafter redistilled at a lower temperature

Sir Cloudesley * a hot beverage of brandy, light beer, lemon juice, spices and sugar

sirocco * a malting kiln used in the distillation process

snapdragon * burnt brandy; brandy itself means 'burnt wine'

sotol * a Mexican spirit distilled from the fermented sap of the 'desert spoon' plant

sou'-wester * nautical cant for rum cut with water

spencer * a modest measure of gin, in allusion to its value as a 'life preserver'

spiritualized * infused with, or steeped in, hard liquor

spirituosity * the sublimated, quintessential quality of distilled liquor

spiritus frumenti * whisky, considered the life-essence of grain

spiritus pyroxylicus * aka wood spirit or naphtha; it is toxic if consumed

spiritus rectificatus * 'rectified' or purified drinking alcohol; at around 95% ABV, it is a highly concentrated form of ethanol

spiritus vini gallici * brandy, being the distilled essence of wine

spodiodi * a mixture of generic bar whisky and inferior port popular with beatniks back in the day

spunkie * Scotch whisky or spirituous liquor more broadly

squareface * gin from Germany or Schiedam in Holland, judged to be inferior

stagma * distilled liquor

stalagma * redistilled liquor

stellatour * an obsolete synonym for either a still or a distillery

stengah * an old expat favourite of whisky and soda water in equal measure, over ice

stewed Quaker * burnt rum with butter, formerly taken as a cold remedy

stillatitious * produced by distillation, drop by drop

stillified * distilled

stillroom * historically, a chamber reserved for the preparation of alcoholic cordials

stinkibus * any poor-quality, adulterated spirit drink

stratosphere * Crème Yvette liqueur; as a cocktail, topped with champagne

strip-me-naked * raw, unadulterated gin

strunt * spirituous liquor; an antique Scots term

Stygian liquor * an old term of disapprobation for spirits: think 'demon drink'

surfeit waters * spiced alcoholic cordials once recommended for their digestive qualities following consumption of a hearty meal

switchel * a generic term for cocktails

swizzle-stick * a utensil for whisking or frothing up cocktails; a swizzle is a type of cocktail that is stirred, not shaken

T

taggeen * a measure of Irish whiskey

tarantula-juice * rotgut, or inferior American whiskey

thujone * a chemical compound once thought to be 'la feé verte' herself – the psychoactive property in absinthe

timber-doodle * US slang for distilled drink

titanic * vodka and Mandarine Napoleon mixed in a glass half full of ice cubes

toddyize * to ply or supply with toddy, a traditionally spirit-based hot medicinal drink sweetened with the addition of sugar or honey

toothful * a dram or nip of spirits

torp * powerful domestically distilled liquor; it torpedoes one so

tovarich * a vodka and kümmel liqueur cocktail

trestarig * of whisky, thrice-distilled

tsipouro * rough Cretan raki or native firewater

turbinaceous * peat-flavoured, a taste descriptor for Scotch whisky

twankay * Victorian-era vernacular for gin

U

uscova * whisky; an early anglicized form of 'usquebaugh'

V

vatting * the blending of malt or grain whiskies from various distilleries

vespitro * the 'silent belch', a forgotten brandy liqueur flavoured with anise

visney * cherry brandy liqueur; no longer consumed

vodkatini * a cocktail of vodka and vermouth

W

whiskybae * whisky; a late anglicized form of 'usquebaugh'

whisky-skin * any cocktail containing a dominant proportion of whisky

witblitz * raw South African home-distilled 'white lightning' spirit

wodky * a nineteenth-century variant rendering of vodka

Y

yack-yack bourbon * American moonshine spirit

Yankee particular * a drop of American whiskey sweetened with molasses

Z

zibeeb * a strongly alcoholic Egyptian liqueur made from raisins

zopy * distilled alcoholic drink in general

zubrowka * a category of vodka flavoured with bison-grass stalks

5

ROLL OUT THE BARREL

– BOTTLES, BUTTS & BEVERAGEWARE –

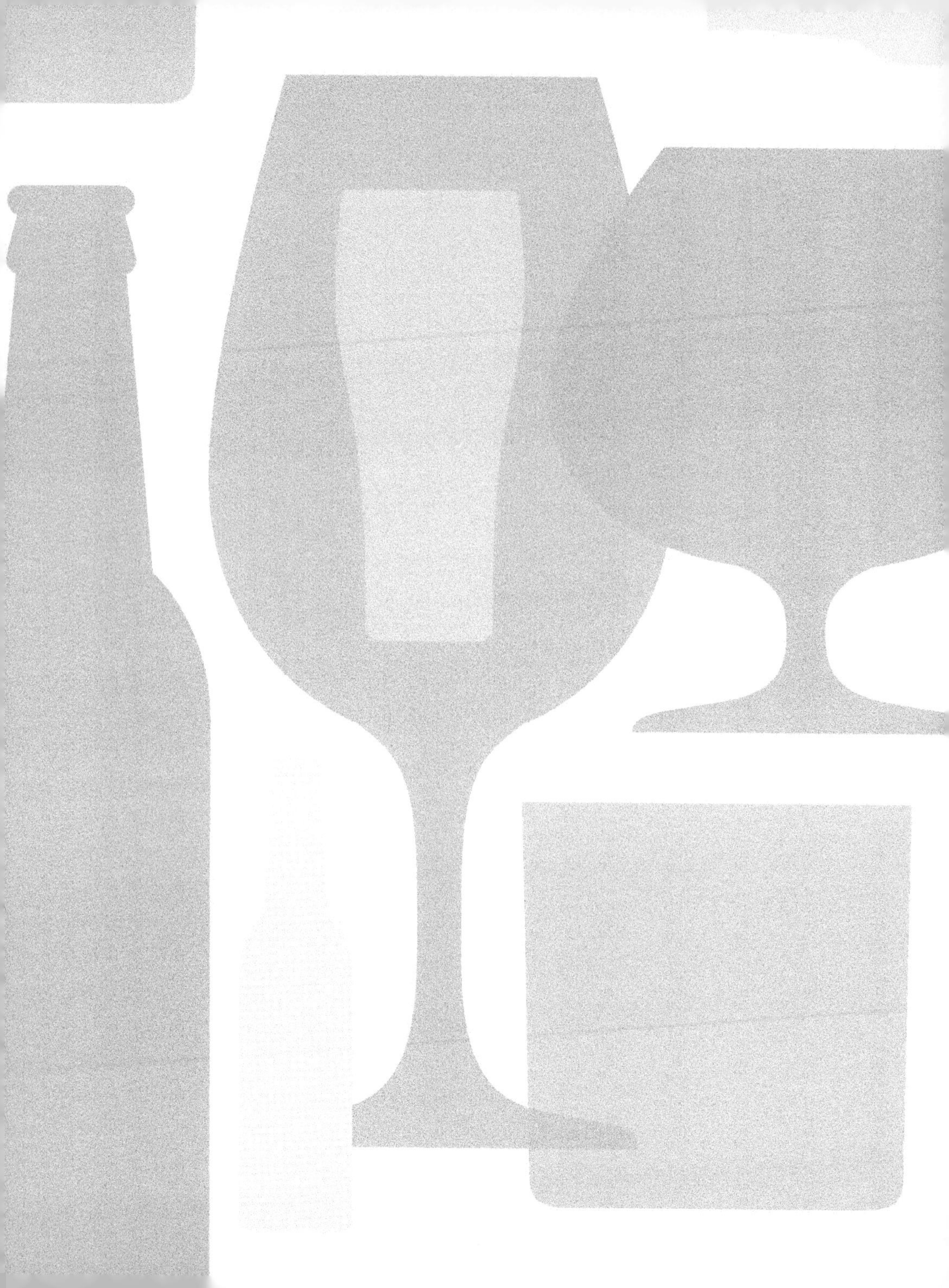

A

abroach * of a liquor barrel – 'on tap', with the contents set to be poured and enjoyed; of the liquor itself – set flowing freely from said barrel

acetabulum * a vinegar bottle or stoppered condiment cup

agrafe * a metal clasp used to fasten the cork in a bottle of effervescent beer or wine

amphora * an ancient two-handled ceramic pitcher for storing and transporting wine

ampulla * a round Roman wine bottle; latterly, a cruet holding consecrated wine

anker * a keg capable of holding ten gallons of brandy

anti-guggler * a tube used to surreptitiously swipe the contents of liquor casks

apostles * the dozen enormous carved casks located in the treasury cellar under Bremen town hall; they contain possibly the oldest potable wine in the world

aristotle * rhyming slang for a bottle

B

balthazar * a 12 litre champagne bottle, with a capacity equivalent to 16 standard bottles

baron * a Belgian beer glass with a half-litre capacity

barrelage * total output of beer expressed or estimated in barrels

barrique * a 225 litre oak barrel used to age Bordeaux wines

beer-bombard * an old leather bottle or jug containing beer

beerness * a cellar or other storage space where beer is kept

bellarmine * a glazed stoneware drinking mug with rounded belly and narrow neck

benjamin * a speciality Belgian beer-tasting glass

berkemeyer * a robust glass similar to a rummer but with a funnel-shaped mouth

beverageware * collectively, the vessels and utensils used for consuming drinks

bidon * a canteen for wine or water

bierstiefel * a German novelty 'beer boot'

bocksbeutel * a dark-green wine bottle with flattened, rounded body originating in Franconia; it currently enjoys the status of a protected bottle shape under EU law

borachio * a wineskin or large leather wine bottle, once common throughout Spain

bottlery * a brewery's bottling department

braga-beaker * a cup in which a person's good health is toasted with fine wine

brendice * a cup with which to drink to someone's lasting health and happiness

brimmered * describes a drinking vessel filled to the point of overflowing

bunghole * an aperture in the side of a wine barrel through which it is variously filled, emptied and replenished

butlerage * the office of butler, charged with stocking, storing and serving drinks in a medieval household

butt * a cask containing two hogsheads or 126 imperial gallons of wine

buttery * a manorial storeroom from which casked wines and beers were dispensed at dinners and banquets

C

calyx-crater * a shallow drinking bowl from Greek antiquity with tall stem

canette * a tall, cylindrical Swiss-German beer mug of the sixteenth century

cantharus * a deep drinking bowl anciently used in the ritual consumption of wine

cantling * a special trestle for supporting and steadying drinks casks

capsuling * the process of capping or crowning beer bottles

carafe * a narrow-necked glass jar for serving wine or water

catacomb * a recessed compartment located in a wine cellar

cellaragium * a fee once charged for laying wine down in a cellar

cellaret * a small case or cabinet holding liquor bottles and decanters

cellarist * formerly an official in a religious house in charge of the wine store

cellarmanship * the art of racking, conditioning, settling and serving cask ales

chalice * a thick bowl-shaped glass for quaffing Belgian Abbey or Trappist beers

chevalier * a mighty 2.5 litre beer glass

chopine * a Bordeaux wine bottle with modest 250ml capacity

choppin * an old Scots measure of liquid capacity, equivalent to half a pint

churchkey * a utensil for prying the caps from beer bottles

clank-napper * a thiever of clanks, or silver beer tankards

clavelin * a special 620ml bottle for holding Jura region 'yellow wine'

cogueful * a quantity sufficient to fill a cogue, a small wooden cup for supping drams

comical farce * rhyming slang for a glass

congius * a Roman measure or 'shellful' of wine; latterly, the pharmaceutical term for a gallon

cooperage * the casks, tanks or containers used to mature or store wine or beer, collectively

copita * a tulip-shaped style of stemware designed for savouring wine, notably fortified wines such as sherry

Cornelius keg * a multi-gallon stainless steel canister popularly used for kegging home-brewed ales

costrel * an old wooden carrying flask holding wine; suspended from the waist, it often went by the moniker 'pilgrim's bottle'

croze * the groove cut in the staves of a liquor cask to receive the barrel head

cyathus * a ladle used specially for filling wine glasses from a mixing bowl

cyclone * a variety of modern barware

cymaise * an ancient pewter wine jar with spout and handle

D

Darwin stubby * a 2.25 litre bottle of beer, today manufactured principally as a tourist souvenir in Australia

decanter * a stoppered bottle used to serve measures of wine and spirits

delphine * an early modern era drinking vessel fashioned in the shape of a dolphin

demiard * a French half-pint measure of beer

demijohn * a substantial drinks bottle featuring a double-handed wicker case for ease of transport

demi-muid * an oak Rhône Valley wine barrel with a capacity of 600 litres

discask * to broach or draw beverage from the cask

dobbin * a small drinking vessel containing a gill's worth, or quarter pint

dolium * a spherical fired clay jug used to store and transport wine and other goods

doppelstück * a bumper German oak wine barrel holding 2400 litres

dopskal * an old Swedish handled drinking bowl for serving hot brandy

drillopota * a drinking vessel either phallus shaped or with a decorative phallus

drinkware * drinking vessels considered generically as a category or commodity

drynchorn * a medieval English drinking horn

E

envined * of a cellar, well provisioned with wine

ewery * historically, the department of a manorial house responsible for the provision of water and drinkware

F

feuillet * a half-barrel of Burgundy or Chablis wine, both measure and keg

fiasco * a Chianti 'flask' or bottle, traditionally presented in a straw basket

fillette * a 'little girl', being a half-bottle of champagne

firkin * a modest keg of beer holding 72 pints

flagon * a small wooden barrel holding a Somerset farmhand's daily quart of cider

flagonet * a little flagon, or traditional drinks vessel with handle, spout and lid

flute * a tall, slender, stemmed glass especially suitable for serving sparkling wines

fountain * a bar tap for drawing beer or cider from the barrel to the customer's glass

fudder * as per a tun, a vessel holding 252 gallons of wine; the largest of the standard barrel sizes

fustage * collectively the vats, tubs, casks and so forth used to make and store wine

G

galopin * a beer-tasting glass of 150ml or so capacity proffered in French and Belgian bars

gargolette * an earthen cooler for wine or water

gauntress * to mount beer on a gantry, or wooden barrel stand

giraffe * a tall-necked tower for dispensing self-service beer in a bar or pub

glassware * the set, class or range of glass drinking vessels

goblet * a glass or metal drinking vessel featuring a bowl resting on a stemmed foot

goliath * a prestige wine bottle holding some 27 litres; also known as a primat

gönc * a traditional Hungarian oak cask used to age sweet Tokay wine

grayhead * a stoneware jar for the purposes of containing spirituous liquor

growler * a half-gallon jug for taking draught beer-to-go home from a US brewpub

guardevine * variously a wine flask or whisky jar

gyllot * a half-gill measure of alcohol

H

habillage * the foil and wire cork cage used to dress bottles of sparkling wine

halbfüder * a German oak wine barrel or butt with a capacity of 450 litres

hanap * anciently, a precious chalice or ornate goblet from which the principal guests drank on great occasions of state

hemina * especially in Sicily, a half-pint measure or ration of wine

hogshead * a barrel type respectively holding 48 imperial gallons of ale, 54 of beer, 60 of cider or 63 of wine

homerkin * an obsolete measure of beer, equivalent to 75 gallons

I

imperial * a large vessel capable of decanting up to six litres of wine or spirits

ingestar * a former continental wine glass holding somewhat over a British pint

J

jackpot * a quarter-pint measure of strong drink in certain English shires of yore

Jacobite * describes a style of historical drinking glass used for toasting Charles Stuart, the Young Pretender; the receptacle was engraved with a pro-Stuart motto or similar symbology

jarman * a large (quart) or little (pint) container for illicitly sold beer or cider

jeroboam * a double magnum, holding four standard champagne bottles

jigger * a shot glass, or vessel for measuring amounts when mixing such as cocktails

jingle-box * a leather drinking vessel adorned with silver bells, fashionable among roisterers in Elizabethan England

jolly-boys * a set of small drinking vessels connected to one another by tube, fashionable among roisterers in Victorian England

jorum * a large punch bowl

jubbe * an erstwhile outsize container for consuming ale or wine

K

kegerator * a storage unit for dispensing cool draught beer

kilderkin * a small barrel of beer holding 18 imperial gallons or 144 pints; occasionally called a kempkin or kinkin

kovsh * a traditional ornate ceremonial Russian mead-drinking vessel or ladle

krateriskos * a small bowl anciently used for diluting wine with water, as was the practice of the time

kylix * a classical Greek wine-drinking vessel; later adopted and adapted as 'chalice'

L

lagenarious * shaped as or styled after a flagon or flask

leaguer * a cask of wine or brandy, roughly equivalent to two hogsheads or a butt

libatory * a vessel for pouring drink offerings to propitiate thirsty deities

limonadier * a corkscrew featuring an integrated bottle opener

longbeard * a long-necked stoneware drinking jug from times past

M

magnum * a double-sized bottle of wine, especially champagne

maximus * a wine bottle with a record capacity of 130 litres or 1200 standard glasses

mazzard * a medieval hardwood drinking bowl inlaid with bands of silver gilt

melchior * a show bottle of champagne, equivalent in capacity to 24 standard bottles

melchizedek * an even larger stunt bottle of champagne, equivalent in capacity to fully 40 standard bottles though seldom containing any liquor at all

methuselah * a quadruple magnum, holding eight standard champagne bottles

middy * an Australian beer glass, intermediate in size between a pony and a schooner

miniature * a small bottle containing 50ml of spirits

monteith * a large silver punch bowl with a scalloped rim for cooling wine glasses

mousseline * a delicate, thinly blown wine glass ornamented like lace or muslin

muller * a vessel for heating alcoholic beverages

muselet * a capped wire 'muzzle' or cage for securing the cork in a bottle of sparkling wine

mutchkin * an old Scottish liquor measure some three-quarters of an imperial pint

N

naggin * a 200ml bottle of spirits, popular in Ireland

nebuchadnezzar * a 15 litre capacity promotional bottle of champagne

nipperkin * a vessel containing a half-pint quantity of wine, ale or spirits

nobbler * a glass for drinking alcohol from, native to Australia and New Zealand

noggin * a small cup holding a gill or quarter-pint measure of liquor

nonic * describes a traditional UK pint glass bevelled near the top to lend extra grip

O

octave * a rare 100 litre wine barrel

oenochoe * anciently, a pitcher used to transfer wine from mixing bowl to cup

oenophorum * either a jug for carrying wine or basket for transporting wine bottles

optic * a device to control the quantity of spirituous liquor dispensed from the bottle

oxhoft * the forerunner of the liquor barrel, corresponding in capacity to a hogshead

P

passglas * a tall cylindrical 'pass glass' or beaker for communal drinking

patera * a classical shallow ceramic or metal libation bowl

phellem * cork, as used as a bottle-stopping piece

piccolo * a quarter-bottle of wine

piggin * a wooden pail for swilling beer from

pigtail * a slender tank-mounted coil used to dispense samples of brewing beer

pint-stoup * a beer tankard

pipot * a liquor measure equivalent to half a pipe or butt

pitcherful * the quantity contained in any large, lipped vessel for pouring drinks

Plimsole line * a rule on a beer glass indicating the full fluid measure

pocket pistol * a hip flask or canteen for spirits

poculum * an ancient Roman drinking cup

pokal * a common European pilsener glass

polypin * a capacious plastic keg popular in home-brewing and the off-trade

porrón * a handle-less flask with narrow grip-neck and tapering spout for drinking Spanish wine, the contents being poured directly into the mouth at an angle

pot-goddardine * a late medieval take on the sturdy drinking goblet

pottle-bottle * a four-pint tankard of ale

Priapus vitreus * a stylized, phallus-shaped drinking vessel

psykter * a metal or earthenware pot used in classical times as a wine cooler

puncheon * a cask with a capacity of 84 gallons, now mostly used for ageing wine

punt * the dimple often found at the bottom of modern wine bottles

pupitre * an A-frame rack used for riddling champagne or storing wine bottles

purchase * the thumbpiece or rest found on the handle of a beer tankard

Q

quadrantal * a Roman liquid measure corresponding to roughly six gallons or 48 pints of wine

quaich * a Scottish shallow two-handled drinking bowl used for formal toasts

quartern * a synonym for a gill, or quarter-pint measure of liquor

qvevri * a traditional Georgian earthenware wine jar, often buried underground, in which the contents are allowed to ferment and age

R

rehoboam * a treble magnum, holding six standard champagne bottles

rhyton * an ancient Greek drinking horn used to offer libations to the gods

rickhouse * a warehouse for ageing barrels of bourbon

Rodney * a wine decanter with a wide, heavy base for use on board ships

rummer * a goblet for quaffing wine or beer, cylindrical in body and ovoid in mouth

rundlet * an old, irregular wine cask containing one-seventh the capacity of a butt

S

sabrage * the act of opening a wine or champagne bottle with the flourish of a sword

sack-butt * a large wine cask or wineskin

salmanazar * a nine-litre champagne bottle, with a capacity equivalent to 12 standard bottles

sarcophagus * a wine cooler

schooner * a popular Australian lager glass, most commonly holding 400ml

seau * an ice bucket for serving chilled wine

seidel * a solid handled mug holding up to half a litre of beer

sester * an old pitcher measure – 3-4 gallons for wine and 12 for beer and ale; a sester-penny was a duty levied on such quantities of liquor produced

sextary * a Roman pint measure of wine, or one-sixth of a congius

Shaftesbury * an old gallon pot with tap, used to serve wine

shakerful * the contents or quantity contained within a cocktail shaker

shetland * a petite Australian 'pony' beer-tasting glass holding four fluid ounces

shooper * a large American beer glass

simpulum * historically, a long-handled ladle used to taste and pour offertory wine

singleton * a corkscrew

skinking-pot * a vessel from bygone days for filling a carafe with wine

skylight * the portion of a glass remaining empty once the drink has been poured in

skyphos * a deep, two-handled ancient Mycenaean wine cup

snifter * an American brandy glass, wide in body and narrower towards the lip

snorkel * at two US fluid ounces, a micro-measure of beer for sampling purposes

solomon * a wine bottle holding 20 litres

sovereign * a wine bottle holding 25 litres

spigot * a barrel peg or plug; alternatively, a beer tap or faucet

sponage * the practice of securing or tightening wine casks using chips

steinkrug * a 'stone jug' forerunner of the traditional German ceramic beer stein

stelvin * a style of screwcap wine top

stemware * collectively, drinking vessels featuring a stem supporting a bowl

stillion * a cruciform cradle used to support wooden vats in a brewery or pub cellar

T

tallboy * a tall-stemmed glass or goblet

tankard * traditionally a stout pewter beer mug, often with a hinged lid

tantalus * a decorative stand or case holding a set of cut-glass wine decanters

tanzemann * an old Swiss drinking vessel made from ornately sculptured wood

tappit-hen * a jar with a distinctive knobbed lid, holding three quarts of Scotch

tastevin * a shallow silver wine-sampling utensil

tea-canister * an old cant term for a brandy flask

temperer * a drinks bowl, especially for mixing wine with water

tersail * also known as a tierce, a wine cask with one-third the capacity of a butt

tertian * a wine cask holding 84 gallons, or double the capacity of the tersail

thermopotis * a wine-warming vase from ancient times

thirdendeal * a proud pewter flagon containing three pints of ale

timothy * a dram glass or modest toddy bowl

tokkori * a special bottle for warming saké

tonneau * a supersized cask holding 900 litres of wine; in the wine trade, also a shipment of 100 cases carrying 1200 regular bottles

tregnum * a bottle holding 2.25 litres of port wine

triental * a drinking vessel one-third the volume of a Roman pint or sextarius

tub * a four-gallon container for illicit spirits, in both old English smuggler and modern American Prohibition vernacular

tulip * a beer glass shaped so as to preserve both the head and aroma of the brew

tumbler * originally a cup which would remain upright only if emptied – so encouraging the drinker to drain the precious fluid without delay

tunc * the solid base common to certain beer glass styles, lending stability and heft

tunnery * a facility where tuns – large casks of wine or ale – are filled and stored

tyg * an antiquarian multi-handled communal drinking mug made of pottery

U

unstoppered * with plug, seal, cork or bung removed from the vessel or container

unullaged * of a cask, unaffected by contents loss through leakage or evaporation

urceolus * a small single-handed Roman pitcher used for serving wine at table

V

valincher * a special implement for sampling sherry from ageing casks, otherwise variously known as a venencia, valentia or vellinch

vatful * sufficient in volume to fill a vat or tun, in particular regard to beer or cider

venenciador * one practised in the customary use of the valincher

viertel * in Germany and Austria, a quarter-litre measure of beverage, notably wine, or a vessel containing such a measure

vinager * a large wine container

vintry * a wine cellar or storehouse for wines

W

weeper * a wine bottle displaying early signs of a defective cork; alternatively, a beer barrel leaking due to faulty staves

whiskin * a shallow drinking vessel for the consumption of strong liquor

widget * a device inserted into cans or bottles of beer to generate a frothy head when poured, in imitation of the draught product

wiederkom * a tall, coloured or even painted drinking glass popular in Germany

willybecher * a standard German beer tumbler

wineskin * a receptacle made from goat's hide for carrying wine on a journey

winston * a wine bottle holding 600ml

Y

yard of ale * a trick beer glass with trumpet mouth, long, narrow neck and globular body; often reserved for drinking challenges owing to its daunting capacity

Yukon mickey * a copious frontier bottle of spirits

Z

zegedine * a Hungarian silver drinking cup

6

LIQUID ASSETS

– LICENSED PREMISES & THE DRINKS TRADE –

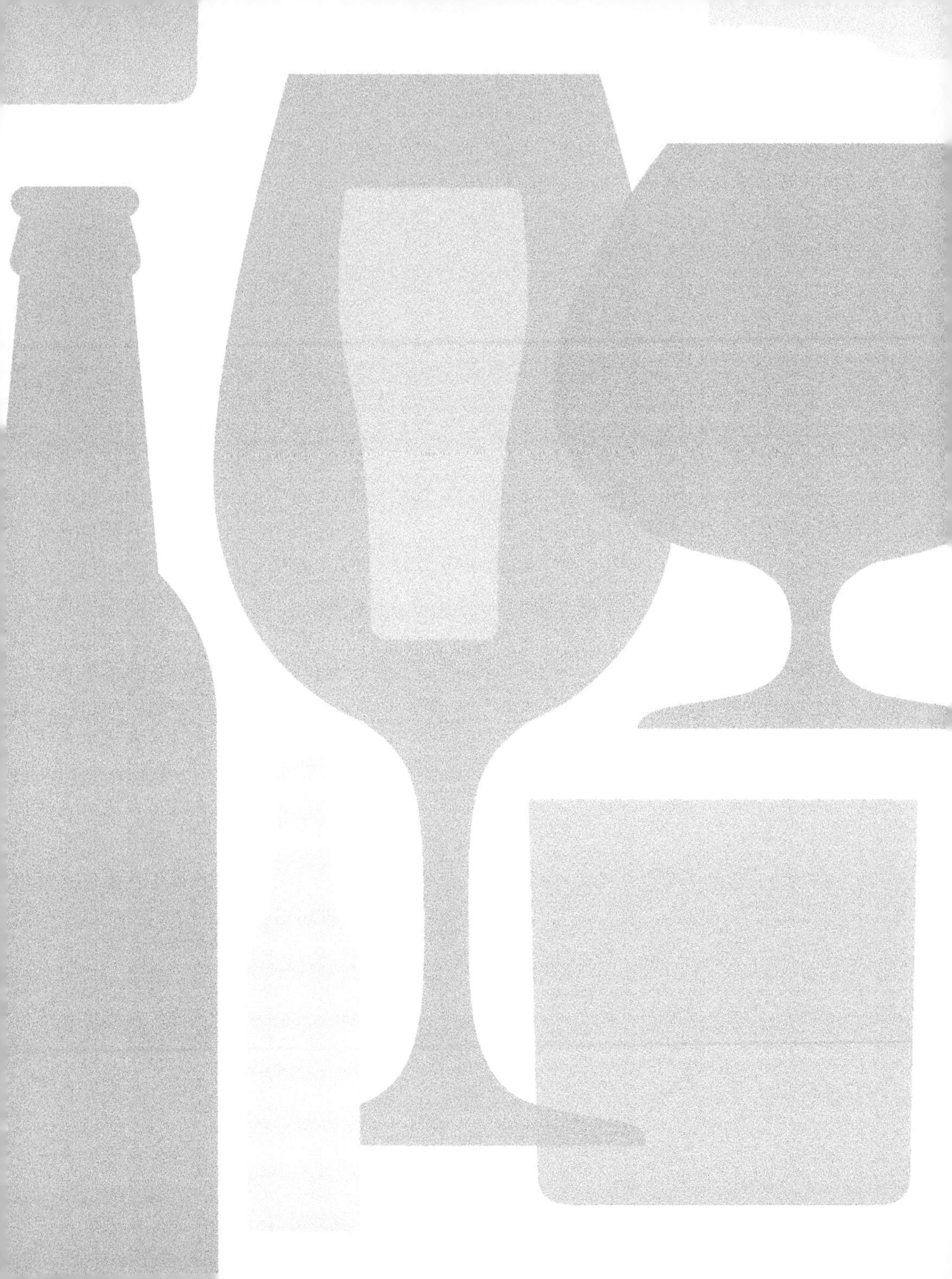

A

Abraham grains * a publican who brews and sells his own beer

abs-lushery * down the boozer's

adrench * to serve with drinks

ale-drapery * the practice or profession of tavern-keeping

ale-score * a bar tab or slate

B

barley-island * an ale-house

barrelhouse * a ramshackle, disreputable saloon-cum-brothel

beerflation * the vertiginous rise in the cost of a humble pint

beer-jerker * a bartender

beer-jugger * a barmaid

beer-monger * an innkeeper

beorsele * an old English beer-hall

bibbery * premises where intoxicating liquor is sold

bibster * one who retails ale

biergarten * a beer-garden, or property licensed for communal al fresco drinking

birling * the selling and serving of strong refreshments

bistrot * a wine-house

blind tiger * a nineteenth-century American illegal drinking saloon

bodega * a specialist wine-bar

Bohemian bungery * a bar much frequented by impecunious writers and artists

boniface * a proprietor of an inn or public house

bootlegging * the illicit overland traffic or trade in excisable alcoholic beverages

boozorium * humorously, a hotel bar-room

bothan * a rural or otherwise remote hut used as an illegal drinking den

brandy-spinner * a merchant dealing in spirituous liquors

brasserie * an up-market beer-house where good food can ordinarily be obtained

brewpub * a craft ale bar with its own attached microbrewery

brewster session * a court-sitting hearing applications for liquor licences

budge kain * an old cant term for a public house

buttling * the practice of selling or serving alcohol

buvette * a modest tavern or refreshment bar

C

caback * an old Russian pot-house or dram-shop

cantina * a Latin American saloon; alternatively, an Italian wine-shop

cocktailian * a master bartender

corkage * a restaurant charge for serving wine bought off-premises

D

delicatessen * a Prohibition-era euphemism for an illicit drinking establishment

diddle-cove * a gentleman who keeps a low gin-house

dispense * a theatre or club bar, especially for staff working on the premises

dram-shop * a small, spartan bar chiefly selling measures of spirits to go

drenchus * the oldest word in the English language for a tavern or public house

drinkdom * the drinks trade, especially with reference to its commercial power and influence

drinkery * a liquor store; not to be confused with a 'drunkery', or public house

drink-silver * money set aside, or awarded as a perquisite, for spending in a tavern

Dutch doggery * a cheap, squalid saloon

E

enoteca * a wine-bar

estaminet * a modest bar or café

F

fizzical culturalist * jocularly, a bartender or cocktail-maker

G

Ganymedean * a barman or pot-boy, one who pours drinks and collects glasses

gargle-factory * a vernacular expression for a public house

gasthaus * a German-style inn or tavern

gastropub * a bar serving high-end beer and food

gin-palace * any lavishly or gaudily fitted-out pub in the late Victorian style

gobleter * a cup-bearer; one who serves liquor at table

goth * a community-interest public house where responsible drinking is encouraged, with the consumption of spirits in particular closely regulated

guzzery * a very basic, no-frills boozer

H

haberdasher * an old humorous term for a publican as a dealer in 'tape' or spirits

hatchetation * a protest attack on licensed premises against the perceived moral iniquity of selling intoxicating liquor

haustor * an ancient Roman sommelier

heuriger * an Austrian wine-tavern selling the latest local vintage

hostelaphily * the collection of tavern signs and boards; a hobbyist's pursuit

howff * a traditional Scottish watering-hole

I

innholder * a person licensed to sell beer with entertainment on the premises

ivy-garland * an outdoor inn sign showing that wine is available to purchase inside

izakaya * a casual Japanese drinking-shop, especially popular with those seeking after-work refreshment; kanpai!

J

jointist * mine host of an illicit saloon

K

kaniker * formerly, an ale-house keeper

kapelion * anciently, a tavern

kiddleywink * an old Cornish or West Country ale-house

knight of the spigot * a mock-heroic moniker for a tapster or publican

L

liquordom * a nonce-word for the drinks industry or interest

lushery * informally, a public house

lust-house * a German or Dutch tavern with its own beer-garden

M

max-ken * a gin-house, max being eighteenth-century slang for 'mother's ruin'

meduwong * the grounds of an Anglo-Saxon mead-hall

mixologist * a barman skilled in the art of preparing cocktails

mugroom * an Edwardian tavern admitting only men and serving only stouts and ales

N

neo-speakeasy * a hipster cocktail bar

nickum * a novice ale-house keeper or vintner

nip joint * an unlicensed Appalachian establishment selling moonshine booze

O

off-licensee * a proprietor of a liquor store

ordinary * an inn of the American colonial period purveying meals at a fixed price alongside wine and ales

ouzeria * a traditional Greek tavern serving ouzo and bar snacks

P

phuza-cabin * a South African shebeen

pincern * a drinks servant or attendant

pocillation * the act of waiting upon or serving drinkers

popinal * pertaining to bars; pubbish

popinjay * a traditional tavern sign

porterhouse * premises where porter and other malt liquors are served

posadaship * tavern-keeping, notably in Spain or a Spanish-speaking country

potboydom * bartenders regarded as a collectivity or class

pot-housey * pub-like

pourboire * a gratuity offered to waiting staff literally 'for a drink' for themselves

prisage * a former customs impost levied upon wines imported into England

propination * a historical trading monopoly on the right to manufacture, distribute and sell alcoholic beverages

pubco * in the UK, a company owning a chain of 'tied' public houses

publicanism * the business of owning or managing a bar

pulqueria * a Mexican bar-room, especially one serving the local pulque brew

punch-house * historically, an Indian tavern popular with sailors on shore leave

purl-boat * a vessel from which herb-infused ale was formerly sold on the Thames

Q

qualifier * one who assesses the quality and strength of alcoholic beverages for public consumption

queer-bluffer * a cut-throat innkeeper

R

rathskeller * a traditional German basement beer-hall

red-lattice * relating to or appropriate to an ale-house

reductionist * one who favours restricting the award of public drink licences

rubbity-dub * antipodean slang for a public house

Rum Row * a city neighbourhood notorious for its seedy bars and street alcoholics

rum-running * the smuggling of contraband booze by water

S

sagittary * a common tavern sign from times past

saloon smasher * one who practises or encourages the wrecking of public houses in protest at the drinks trade and its baleful influence on public health and morals

shebang * a western saloon

shebeen queen * in South Africa, a female hostess of a bar where illicit liquor is purveyed

shenker * a regular tavern keeper or bartender

shoful * a lower-class drinking establishment

shot-shark * a tavern waiter

shypoo * a drinks establishment retailing second-rate liquor

siwash * to prohibit someone from buying alcohol

sluicery * one of a myriad slang terms for a public house

sly-grogster * one who sells excisable liquor without licence

snuggery * a bar-parlour, set off from and generally quieter than the main room

sommelier * a wine steward or waiter

sot's-hof * a low bar regarded as a haunt of drunkards

speakeasy * an underground drinking establishment during the Prohibition years

spicket-wench * a barmaid

squeaker * a bar-boy or drinks servant

squire of the gimlet * either bartender or publican

steelyard * a wine-house; historically, one situated on the north bank of the Thames in the environs of Tower Bridge

suck-casa * a former cant term for a public house

su-pouch * a female innkeeper

swamper * a jack of all trades employed in a saloon

swillery * informally, a hotel with a popular public bar

T

tabernarious * pertaining to taverns

tankard-yeoman * one who serves liquor

tapstership * bartending as a profession

tapstry * a room where draught beer is drawn or 'tapped' for customers

taverning * the keeping or owning of a licensed inn or tavern

tavernry * tavern expenses, or drinks money

teetotum * a temperance inn, or restaurant serving only non-alcoholic beverages

thermopolite * an innkeeper, or owner of a wine-shop

thermopolium * in antiquity, a tavern selling hot liquor, notably mulled wine

thermopoly * the business of keeping a public house

thirst-aid station * an American comic colloquialism for a liquor store or bar

tippling * tavern-keeping or otherwise dispensing strong drink

Tom-and-Jerry * a drinking-house of rough reputation

trantery * the retailing of ales and beers

U

under-skinner * a junior bartender

V

versor * a cup-bearer, or one who attends at the drinks table

vintnery * the occupation of a wine merchant or tavern keeper

W

whistling-shop * an illicit prison dram-shop

winbrytta * a purveyor of wines in Anglo-Saxon times

wobble-shop * an establishment where intoxicants are sold without licence

Z

zinc * a bar counter

7

OMNES BLOTTO

– DRINKING & DRUNKENNESS –

A

acataposis * a pathological inability to ingest liquor or liquids in any form

adipsy * an abnormal absence of thirst, extending to antipathy for drinking itself

alabandical * coarsened by the effects of strong drink; boorish in booze

alcoholiday * an extended period of leisure passed in recreational boozing

alcoholophilia * a weakness for intoxicating liquor

allicholy * maudlin and melancholic with drink

altogethery * somewhat tipsy

anacreontic * a drinking song celebrating conviviality and boon companionship

antiposia * a morbid reluctance or outright refusal to drink

auto-brewery syndrome * an anomalous medical condition whereby intoxicating quantities of ethanol ferment within the gut from ingested carbohydrates

B

bacchanalia * a drunken revel, classically in honour of Bacchus, Roman god of wine

bacchanalize * to embark on a roistering drinking spree

bacchation * an instance of riotous drunkenness

Bacchi plenus * blazing drunk on wine

barleyhood * a foul mood or temper induced by drinking

barm-feast * a festive get-together over many beers or ales

beerienteering * a competitive pub crawl with a challenge awaiting at each watering-hole

beerified * inebriated on beer

beernoculars * night-vision goggles imagined to activate after several pints, making even the ordinarily unattractive sexually appealing to the eye of the 'wearer'

befuddlement * intoxication; fuddle itself is an archaic synonym for alcohol

betipple * to befuddle with drink

bever * a time for drinking

bezzling * quaffing to excess

bibamus papaliter! * a toast meaning 'Let's drink like a pope!'; after Benedict XII, who earned a certain notoriety for his enjoyment of fine wine

bibation * plain old boozing

bibativeness * a term from the discredited discipline of phrenology denoting an innate constitutional fondness for consuming beverages of all kinds

bibbership * dilettante drinking

bibesy * an ardent impulse to drink

bibitory * pertaining to drinking

bibosity * the capacity to consume outrageous quantities of alcohol

bibulate * to enjoy a tipple or three

bibulous * hard-drinking

blindo * a heavy drinking session

blitzkrieged * thoroughly blasted or drunk

bonally * to raise one's charged glass and wish a departing guest Godspeed

boozefest * an event or party where drink is liberally provided

boozeroo * an antipodean drinking spree

boozify * to drink with the full intention of getting drunk

boskiness * the quality of being muddled with drink

bottle-swagger * pot-valour, or more colloquially 'Dutch courage'

bowsered * all liquored-up

Brahms & Liszt * in rhyming slang, bladdered

brandified * sodden with brandy

brannigan * a drinks binge

brimmer * to drink intoxicating beverages with abandon

brindize * to drink to someone's good health

brutify'd * beastly drunk

bumbaste * to drain the glass dry, glass after glass

bybbe * to sneak sips of strong liquor at frequent intervals

C

campaniled * rare old American campus slang meaning 'all lit up' with drink

canteen medal * a stripe awarded for consuming a heroic quantity of alcohol

capernoity * bemused with booze

carbo-load * to drink beer, in campus slang

carousal * a drinking bout in company

chateaued * a society euphemism for being squiffy with wine

chemically inconvenienced * a PC euphemism for being inebriated

cherry-merry * half-way drunk

cherubimical * beatifically blotto

chloroformed * insensible with drink

chopin * to tipple

chug-a-lug! * an exhortation to gulp a drink down without pausing until consumed

ciderspace * a nonce-word explained as 'the virtual multidimensional world inhabited by tramps'

citroned * indisposed through drinking citron water, a cordial made from lemon peel

cockers-p * a society term for a cocktail party

cocktailed * under the influence of one too many cocktails

columbered * an old cant term meaning drunk and incapable

comboozelated * a modern campus term meaning drunk and incapable

compotationship * drinking in company

comus * a drinking bout; after Comus, son of Bacchus and god of drunken excess

cottabus * an ancient Greek drinking game featuring wine dregs flung at targets

crapulency * intemperate drunkenness

crapulosity * a tendency to intemperate drunkenness

cupshodden * drunk; in one's cups

cupstantial * substantially drunk

curjute * to overthrow the senses through strong drink

curwhibbles * a Newfoundland regionalism for the drunken staggers

D

debacchate * to rage or rampage drunkenly

decks-awash * figuratively soaked in alcohol

delibate * to sip or sup, savouring the taste

dingbatisis * informally, hard drinking

dionysiac * orgiastically drunk; after Dionysos, Greek god of wine and revelry

doundrins * afternoon drinking

dramming * hitting the spirits bottle

driffling * overindulging in alcohol

drinkative * inebriated, or with a predilection for being so

drink-drowned * thoroughly stewed in drink

drink-hail * historically, a customary response to a drinking pledge or 'wassail'

drinking-do * an instance of drunken merry-making

drinkitite * a humorous term for thirst, playfully complementing 'appetite'; 'on the drinkitite' formerly meant to be on an alcoholic spree

drouthy * thirsty; hence, by euphemistic extension, fond of drinking intoxicating beverages

druncenscipe * old English drunkenness

drunkalog * a drunken dialogue, or narrative regarding drinking

drunkardize * to behave in the manner of a drunkard

drunkelewness * having a propensity to drunkenness

drunkify * to make drunk

dwile flonking * a pub sport involving teams dancing to avoid being struck by a 'dwile' or beer-soaked cloth thrown by their opponents – allegedly

dyskataposis * great difficulty or discomfort in swallowing drink

E

ebibe * to drink dry, to the very dregs

ebriety * intoxication

ebrilagnia * sexual desire inflamed by the effects of alcohol

epotation * the practice of imbibing to excess

F

flagonal * having enjoyed several jars of beer or ale

flatch-kennurd * half-drunk, by back-formation

flustrated * agitatedly the worse for drink

fogmatic * with one's faculties impaired through drink

foozlified * dazed and confused by intoxicating beverages

fordrunken * quite exhausted or burnt out with drinking

fou * displaying distinct signs that one has had one's fill of drink for the evening

frommeling * the dumb-ass drunken wheeze of smashing a fizzed-up beer can against the forehead until it sprays open

frontloading * tanking up on cheap drink before heading off for the night's revelry

G

gambrinous * all beered-up

gebeorscipe * Anglo-Saxon beer-drinking

genevaed * pickled in genever, or Dutch gin

gilravage * to participate in a bout of riotously intemperate eating and drinking

ginnified * stupefied with gin

glowsing * drinking freely

grapeshot * addled on wine

groatable * intoxicated; a groat, or fourpence, was once the standard price of a drink

groggified * partially drunk

guttle * to drink immoderately

H

hausture * the act of drinking up

hicksius doxius * tipsified

hobbernobbering * the practice of clinking glasses together when drinking toasts

hyperposia * the consumption of drink or any other fluid in excessive volumes

I

ikkinomi * 'down in one', a Japanese company or campus drinking challenge-cum-initiation

imbibition * the act of tippling

impixlocated * thoroughly inebriated

impotant * not drinking

impote * to drink heavily

inabstinent * regularly partaking of strong drink

incognitibus * non compos mentis with liquor

indrunken * to ply another with drink

inebriacy * a state of persistent drunkenness

inebriation * a state of present drunkenness

inebrious * copiously or constantly drunk

insobriety * tipsiness

inter pocula * over drinks

intoxicated * literally 'poisoned' with alcohol

invertebrated * legless with liquor

irrigate * humorously, to wet one's parched lips with alcohol

ishkimmisk * as per 'skimished', Shelta cant for drunk

ivresse * a state of exalted drunkenness

J

jollify * to make tipsy; a jollo is an Australian drinking party

jubilated * drunk through over-celebration

jug-bitten * inebriated

juggins-hunting * looking for a patsy to stand you a drink or pick up your bar tab

K

kastenlauf * 'crate-running', a central European team drinking-race

kegging * buying booze for consumption elsewhere, as in a neighbouring dry area

kelty mends * an obligation of an extra drink, imposed as 'punishment' for lagging behind others at the bar

khamriyya * a pre-Islamic genre of Arabian wine poetry

komastic * pertaining to the 'komos', a parodic drunken procession often performed on the classical Greek stage, whence 'comedy'

L

langerated * languishing in a state of mellow intoxication

lechayim! * a drinking salutation, literally 'to life!'

liquidation * the action of imbibing alcoholic drink

liquorishness * a fondness, perhaps overfondness, for intoxicating drink

liquor-seasoned * pickled in drink

locus * to render insensibly drunk, especially by spiking another's drink

longwhiskey * drunk, in pidgin English

lubricated * well-oiled with strong drink

lurrep * to swallow liquor with great vigour

lustick * jovial in drink

M

madza-beargered * half-drunk

mallemaroking * drunken carousing aboard icebound Greenland whaleships

malt-inspired * in transports of drunken delight

marinated * soused with drink

Martin-drunk * to be so exceedingly drunk as to paradoxically be sober again

maudlinize * to make sentimentally lachrymose with drink

meduburg * 'meadsville'; an old English town with a reputation for enjoying its mead

methodistconated * a Prohibition-era coinage meaning intoxicated

Missae de Potatoribus * irreverent 'masses for drinkers', celebrated in medieval times by a movement of bibacious clerical satirists known as the goliards

moroculous * drunk in Glasgow

mortallious * profoundly drunk

muckibus * effusively emotional with drink

mulvathered * lathered in alcohol

mustulent * intoxicated on wine

muzzling * drinking heartily

N

nazy * mildly drunk; squiffy

neknominate * to film oneself drinking in an offbeat fashion before posting the feat on social media and passing on the challenge

nestoposia * the act of taking alcohol on an empty stomach

nimptopsical * pleasantly inebriated

O

obfusticated * humorously, bewildered or bamboozled with drink

oenolagnia * wine-induced lust

oenophlygia * a state of wine-inspired drunken abandon

omnibibulous * capable and inclined to drink anything alcoholic

omnipotans * in medical humour, determinedly and indefatigably 'all-drinking'

oxycrocium * 'plastered' drunk

P

palatic * paralytically drunk

palintoshed * plain drunk

paroinia * frenzied or violent intoxication, especially where wine is the cause

peloothered * a Joyceanism meaning incapacitated with drink

pepst * in a state of inebriation

periodics * a regular drinking spree or bender

perpendicular drinking * a passing tradition of hard drinking standing at the bar, in the absence of table service or even of basic pub amenities such as tables and chairs

perpotation * an instance of extended, excessive drinking; a binge

philanthropissed * a nonce-word meaning drunk on someone else's charity

Pillahuana * 'Drunkenness of Children' – a quadrennial Aztec festival where the infant participants were made to imbibe pulque, the Aztec drink of the gods

pipe-merry * happily under the influence of wine

pitcher-praise * the practice of toasting with drinks

pixilated * intoxicated; away with the proverbial fairies

poculary * a medieval pardon or indulgence granted for drinking alcohol

poculation * quaffing; boozing

polydipsia * drinking to excess to slake an insatiable 'thirst'

popination * bar-hopping

potation * the act of drinking, especially to excess

potatory * given to immoderate drinking

pot-companioning * drinking in good company

pot-proof-armour * a plea in mitigation on account of one being drunk

pot-punishment * in humour, compulsory tippling; a harsh penalty indeed

potsmitten * of a deal, concluded by the parties clinking their drinking glasses together

pottical * lyrical in liquor

potulent * moderately inebriated

potvaliantry * drink-induced bravery or belligerence

pot-vertigo * loss of balance or giddiness attendant on heavy drinking

preimbibe * to drink beforehand, in advance of later, more sustained carousing

proface! * a drinking pledge; bottoms up!

propine * to toast or salute in drinking

Province of Bacchus * a state of insobriety

pseudodipsomania * chronic drunkenness in the absence of alcoholic compulsion

Q

quafftide * a time or season for drinking

quaught * to drink deeply; to drain the glass

R

ramsquaddled * an old American colloquialism meaning thoroughly drunk

reswill * to return greedily to the bottle

rivo! * an exhortation or encouragement to drink

rorty * obstreperous with drink

rouzy-bouzy * boisterously drunk

S

sack-sopt * steeped in sack, or strong export wine

sackwah * any location popular as a haunt for illicit drinking

sakazuki * a formal saké-drinking session

savoir boire * knowing how to drink with the appropriate sensibility and style

sconcing * an old varsity tradition requiring a tankard of ale be polished off as penalty for some infraction of etiquette

Scotch by absorption * overly fond of Scotch whisky

scuttered * drunkenly loquacious

semibousy * half-drunk; tipsy

shellacked * 'plastered' with strong drink

shickerhood * inebriation

sipple * to tipple slowly or take frequent small sips at one's leisure

skew-whiff * somewhat squiffy with drink

skoaling * drinking to copious cries of 'cheers!'; in Scandinavia 'skoles' were originally drinking vessels sculpted from the skulls of enemies slain in combat

sky-wannocking * an al fresco drunken frolic

slainte! * a Gaelic drinking salutation

slopping-up * a tramp drinking binge

snapsvisa * a Scandinavian drinking song

snoozamorooed * unconscious with drink; passed-out pissed

sobriety-deprived * a euphemism for drunk, spoofing politically correct speech codes

sooming * avidly drinking a long draught of liquor with a loud sucking noise

sorbillate * to bib or sup alcoholic beverage

sorbition * the action of sipping or imbibing

sosselled * soused in alcohol

sottishness * a predilection for drinking to excess

spifflicated * somewhat tipsy

squeans * cartoon starbursts or bubbles above a character's head denoting intoxication

St Lubbock * a drunken riot

stiefeltrinken * a German party game involving necking beer from glass boots

stinko paralytico * so insensibly drunk the fumes are oozing from every pore

stocious * deeply intoxicated

stonkering * the action of quaffing alcoholic beverages

suction * drinking capacity

sundowner * a summer evening's drinks party

superbibe * to consume a second or subsequent drink

swattle * to imbibe to excess

swilliking * inebriated

swinking * drinking with great effort and energy

symbelwlonc * drunk, in Old English money

symposium * literally, a 'drinking party'

T

tanglefooted * drunk on cheap liquor, especially bootleg Scotch

tavern-discourse * pub talk

tavernize * to regularly patronize public houses

temulency * a propensity for drunkenness

temulentive * routinely inebriated

tight as Andronicus * punningly plastered

Tipperary * tipt, or drunk

tipple square * drunkenly

tipsification * a degree of moderate inebriation

tired & emotional * euphemistically under the influence of alcohol; an expression employed in the scandal sheets to avoid legal action for defamation of character

titubancy * a state of tipsiness

titubant * reeling on one's feet with drink

Tom-and-Jerryism * antisocial drinking

toperism * a proclivity for ingesting intoxicants

tosspotlike * in a drunken fashion

tosticated * intoxicated

toxified * mightily inebriated

trillil * to drink noisily, as with a slurp

U

uphale * to polish off one's drink with great gusto

upsy Dutch * in a hard-drinking fashion

V

varnished * figuratively 'glazed' or glassy-eyed with drink

vinolence * drunkenness attendant on wine-bibbing

vinomadefied * figuratively 'soaked' or 'saturated' in wine

von-blinked * blind drunk

vulcanized * rubber-legged with drink

W

wassailry * the practice of raising a glass of alcohol in toast or celebration

water intoxication * inebriation as a result of one's water supply being spiked with alcohol

waterlogged * nautical slang for drunk

waterloo * to overcome or overpower with drink

waughting * drinking lustily and freely

wazzocked * intoxicated

whemmel * to drink deeply, leaving nary a drop

whiskified * bemused with whisky or a like spirituous liquor

whisky-fair * a gathering of ardent souls to consume ardent spirits

whiskyish * having an unquenchable thirst for whisky

wineathlon * a fun-run punctuated with pit-stops to sample wines

Y

ydrunken * addled of yore

yill * to ply or entertain with ale

Z

zapoy * a Russian bender of two days' or more duration

zigzag * drunk; military slang from the Great War

8

ALCOHOLICS SYNONYMOUS

– A TREASURY OF TOPERS & TIPPLERS –

A

absintheur * a devoted drinker of absinthe

Admiral of the Narrow Seas * one who vomits at the table from drunkenness – and onto his neighbour's lap, no less

alcoholist * an advocate of the liberty to enjoy intoxicating liquor and fierce opponent of prohibitionism

alcoholizer * a habitual drunkard

Alderman Lushington * a hardened boozer

ale-knight * a term, used in scorn more than anything, for a frequent tippler

alpha alcoholic * in the taxonomy of the so-called 'disease concept of alcoholism', one whose dependence is psychological rather than physical

arbiter bibendi * a former master of the Roman revels, whose duty it was to arbitrate on the ratio of water to wine served to guests at the banquet

artilleryman * pre-World War One slang for a volatile and vituperative drunkard – one given to 'outbursts'

B

bacchant * a drunken orgiast; an alcoHoly Roller

barfly * a virtual denizen of seedy drinking dens

barleycap * a confirmed tippler

beer-bibber * one known to be fond of his or her pint

beer-buzzer * a barhound always opportunistically on the lookout for a free beer

beerhood * beer drinkers considered as a class or collectivity

bevvy omee * a drunkard, in Polari argot

bezzler * one with a reputation for drinking to excess

biberon * a fine toper

bibulant * a frequent imbiber

bingo-mort * a woman regularly found under the influence of brandy

blow-bowl * the oldest recorded word in English for an alcoholic or habitual drunkard, attested to 1530

bombard * a heavy drinker

boozician * an affectionate Australian colloquialism for a drunkard

bottle-crony * a boon boozing buddy

brandy-shunter * a retailer or regular heavy consumer of brandy

brother bung * a fellow, indeed fraternal, tippler; also slang once for a brewer

C

cerevisaphile * a beer buff

Champagne Charley * one who is only ever seen drinking the best of fizz

chunder bunny * an inexperienced drinker who cannot yet hold their liquor

ciderist * a cider connoisseur

circumcellion * an itinerant haunter of saloons

claret-cunner * a cognoscente of the finest claret

clareteer * one who much enjoys their red wine

clurichaun * a 'walking thirst', or dipsomaniacal leprechaun

co-alcoholic * a person such as a partner who facilitates another's alcoholism and engages in denial by assuming their daily responsibilities

compotator * a drinking companion

copyholder * a pubgoer who contests his bar bill with the landlord

cup-conqueror * a regular drinking acquaintance

D

daffier * a person who is rather partial to 'daffy', or gin

dehorner * a rubbing-alcohol addict

dipsomaniac * a clinical alcoholic

drammist * one who enjoys the comforts of spirituous liquor

drinkeress * a female soak

dronklap * a South African drunkard

drunkship * the company of drunkards

E

emperor * a drunken man, lording it in his cups

epsilon alcoholic * an episodic 'spree drinker'

ethanolic * ward humour for a patient with evident drink problems

F

freeholder * a man whose wife allows him to remain in the pub without curfew

fuddlecap * a drunkard, notably one whose brain is quite muddled with booze

G

ginnums * an old woman overly fond of strong drink

gintellectual * the proverbial barstool philosopher

godalier * a drunken Englishman of dissolute reputation abroad; a term from the late middle ages known the breadth of the continent

grape-monger * a wine drinker, if not outright wino

gulch-cup * one who drinks both greedily and immoderately

guzzle-guts * one with a deep thirst and a drinking capacity to match

H

homo imbibens * man considered as a drinking animal

hophead * one notorious or otherwise noted for their heavy beer consumption

I

imbiber * euphemistically, a sot

imp of the spigot * one who enjoys intoxicating beverages

inebriate * an early medical term for an alcoholic

intemperant * another early medical term for an alcoholic

intoxicator * one who enjoins others to drink

L

lancepresado * a chancer who visits a public house with only pennies in his pocket

libationer * one entrusted with the honour of pouring drink offerings to the gods

liquorhead * a seasoned boozer

locapour * one who partakes only of locally produced wine or beer

lupomaniac * a beer aficionado – the hoppier the beer, the happier the drinker

lushwell * someone regularly encountered in a state of inebriation

M

malty-cove * a man with a reputation for enjoying his beer

master of the wardrobe * a desperado who would pawn the shirt off his own back to raise the price of a drink

meadist * an authority on honey-wine

mealer * one who restricts their intake of alcohol to mealtimes

merulator * a wine drinker

metho * a down-and-out addicted to methylated spirits

morning's draughtman * one known to set himself up for the day with a bracing tot of liquor

multibibe * a toper renowned for their drinking capacity

muscateer * an enthusiast of cheap muscat wine

N

narcomaniac * a person suffering from a pathological craving for alcohol

norwicher * one who unfairly drinks more than half of a shared tankard before passing it on

O

o-be-joyfuller * a happy drunk

oenomaniac * an alcoholic, especially one with an overpowering passion for wine

oenophil * a wine buff

ombibulus * one who will drink everything and anything intoxicating

P

pantagruelist * a jolly tippler

philistine * a coarse and uncivil drunk

philopotes * an ancient Greek carouser or 'lover of drinking sessions'

plonko * an Antipodean alcoholic

polyposist * a frequent heavy drinker

potationist * a person of drunken habits

potisuge * jocularly, one who enjoys their 'suck' or booze

potomaniac * one who cannot function without alcohol

potpanion * a fellow drinker

pot-parliament * an assemblage or set of drinkers

pot-walloper * one who hits the bottle hard

propinatrix * a woman who invites or incites others to drink

Q

Queen of Scotch * an alcoholic gay man

R

rinse-pitcher * an Elizabethan soubriquet for one seldom sober

rummarian * a knowledgeable rum tippler

S

sack-guzzler * one who drinks sweet white wine to excess

sauce-hound * a compulsive drunk

schnappsteufeln * 'schnapps fiends' – rowdy drunks who were the terror of respectable medieval German society

shot-clog * a bar companion who is tolerated only because they are paying for the rounds

shuffler * a sponger who has gained some notoriety for cadging drinks

Silenus * a tipsy person, named after the Greek god of the dance of the wine-press

skimmisher * an alcoholic derelict

slinger * one with a keen taste for cocktails

slop-beg * a term of derision for an abandoned soak who has lost all self-respect

sottefer * a Devonshire drinker, one not infrequently soused in alcohol

spewterer * a crapulent drunkard

St Bibiana * patron saint of hangover sufferers

St Martin * patron saint of drinkers and drunkards

stumblebum * a skid-row dipso

suckerdom * the world of topers and tipplers

swigsby * one well known for his quaffing exploits

swillocks * one commonly found downing intoxicating drink

swipington * an indefatigable lush

swizzler * one who drinks to the very last drop of the glass

symposiarch * a master of drinking ceremonies

symposiast * a participant at a drinking party

T

taverner * an inveterate pubgoer

thermopot * one who favours mulled liquor

thirstington * a 'thirsty soul' or hardened boozer

tippler * a sot; originally, the term referred to a tavern keeper rather than a patron

tipsificator * one who drinks ever so slightly to excess

toperdom * the companionship of drinkers

trusty Trojan * a bosom buddy, especially a fellow drunken reveller and roisterer

tumbrel * a person drunk to the point of vomiting

turps-nudger * one who abuses potent beverages

V

Vice-Admiral of the Narrow Seas * a drunkard who urinates under the table and onto a fellow toper's shoes

vinipote * a consumer of fine wines

vinologist * a connoisseur of fine wines

vintnephilist * a collector of fine wines

W

whetter * one able to consume copious drams of spirituous liquor

whiskey priest * the archetype of the dissolute clerical soak

Y

yal-yottler * an old Yorkshire ale-bibber

yvronke * an Anglo-Norman drunkard

Z

zawker * a West Country fellow known to appreciate a tipple or two

zythophile * one with a learned appreciation of quality ales and beers

9

ALCOHOLOCAUST

– ADDICTION & ABUSE –

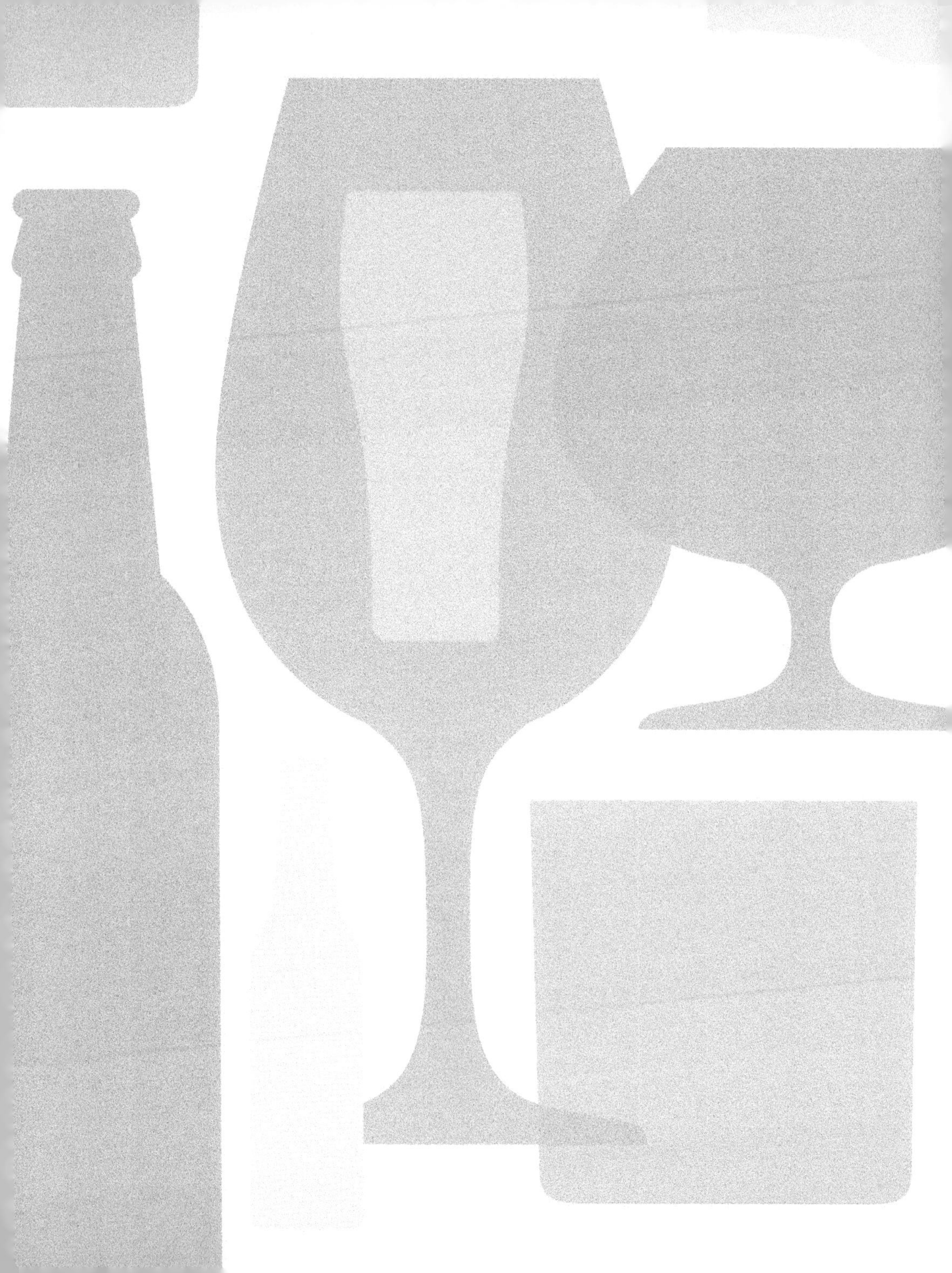

A

absinthism * a disorder formerly attributed to chronic abuse of absinthe, with symptoms ranging from hallucinations to convulsions

acamprosate * a medication widely used to reduce the risk of alcoholic recidivism

acetaldehyde * a by-product of fermentation in the body causing hangovers

acraipala * the class of drugs administered in the management of alcoholism

alcogene * a gene hypothesized as predisposing the carrier to alcohol addiction

alcohol amnestic syndrome * short-term memory loss and compensatory confabulation arising from an established pattern of booze-induced blackouts

alcoholdyscrasia * the characteristic pathology of alcoholism

alcoholic cardiomyopathy * heart failure attendant upon a history of alcohol abuse

alcoholic hallucinosis * the phantasmagorias experienced during drying-out

alcoholic steatohepatitis * fatty liver disease, as classically seen in heavy drinkers

alcoholism * in black humour, 'bourbonic plague'

alcohology * the interdisciplinary study of the impact of alcohol abuse on populations and the social environment

alcoholomania * a harmful obsession with alcohol

alcoholosis * a medico-legal term for alcohol dependency

alcoholpseudoparalysis * a condition characterized by tremor, disturbed motor coordination and anaesthesia caused by overindulgence in intoxicating liquor

alcoholuria * the concentrated presence of ethanol in one's urine

alecy * aberrant or lunatic behaviour under the influence of ale

ale-passion * a hangover induced by excessive consumption of beer

amethysum * any drug believed capable of curing alcoholism

ampelopsin * a plant extract purported to prevent hangovers

antabuse * the redemption of alcoholics by administration of said pioneering drug

antihepatotoxicity * the property of preventing or counteracting liver damage

antlia gastrica * a stomach pump, useful in instances of acute alcohol poisoning

apple-palsy * a signature set of side-effects including paresis, trismus and tremor associated historically with the consumption of home-distilled apple brandy

B

barrel-fever * sickness owing to problem drinking

beer-brussen * grown corpulent from guzzling beer

besotted * in former Alcoholics Anonymous parlance, addicted to intoxication

bibacious * overly fond of strong drink, verging on dependent

bibulosity * pursuing a dangerous relationship with alcoholic beverages

blastophthoria * the hypothetical degeneration of ova or sperm due to alcoholism

brandy-cleek * palsy in the leg as a consequence of sustained spirits drinking

breathalyzer * an instrument measuring blood alcohol concentration, as used to test motorists for suspected drunk-driving

brewer's asthma * humorously, a heavy hangover

brewicide * in morbid humour, drinking oneself to death

bromsulphthalein * a blue dye commonly used in liver function tests

C

cinchonism * quinine poisoning, potentially acquired through excessive consumption of gin and tonic

cirrhogenous * producing cirrhosis of the liver

cirrhosis * the indurated or fibrous condition of a drink-damaged liver

congeners * chemical byproducts of fermentation or distillation, popularly held to be responsible for red wine hangovers

cranberry-eye * a bloodshot or bleary appearance as a result of immoderate drinking

crapula * an early medical term for a hangover

crapulental * physically sick from the over-consumption of alcohol

crawsick * suffering an Irish hangover

D

delirium ebriosorum * severe alcoholic agitation and confusion

detoxification * the process of drying out following sustained alcohol misuse

dihydromyricetin * a chemical compound believed to have a prophylactic effect on ethanol, thereby reducing intoxication and relieving hangover symptoms

dipsomaniacal * dependently craving alcohol

dipsopathy * any diseased or disordered condition caused by heavy alcohol intake

dipsorexia * early stage alcoholism

disintoxication * full restoration to a state of wholesome sobriety

disulfiram * a drug prescribed for its aversive effects in relation to alcohol

drunkensome * addicted to drunkenness

drunkometer * a device for measuring alcoholic intoxication

drunkorexia * the dangerous folly of restricting one's food intake to compensate for calorie accumulation through over-drinking

dyshepatia * disordered liver function

E

ebriection * mental collapse brought on by excessive drinking

ebriosity * a pattern of sustained and habitual drunkenness

F

fetal alcohol syndrome * a spectrum of neurological or physiological disorders and defects afflicting children born to mothers who drank recklessly during pregnancy

formication * in DTs, the hallucinatory sensation of ants crawling over one's skin

THE DRINKTIONARY

G

gallon-distemper * the unpleasant experience of acute alcohol withdrawal symptoms

gamma alcoholism * full physiological and psychological dependence on alcohol

gastric lavage * pumping or purging the stomach of its toxic contents, as in cases of alcohol overdose

grog-blossom * the tell-tale bulbous red nose of a seasoned drinker

H

heebie-jeebies * delirium tremens, as expressed in the idiom of rhyming reduplication

hepatonecrosis * the destruction and death of liver cells

hepatopathy * liver disease

hepatoprotective * acting to prevent or protect against liver damage

hepatotoxic * chemically poisonous or injurious to the liver, as per alcohol

hovenia * a tree whose herbal extract has traditionally been taken as a hangover cure

hyperalcoholaemia * a dangerously high level of ethanol in the bloodstream

I

icterohepatitis * inflammation of the liver with notable jaundice, frequently symptomatic of sustained alcohol misuse

impotentia alcoholica * a chronic case of 'brewer's droop'

inebriism * the scientific study of habitual drunkenness and alcoholism

intemperancy * an early medical yet somewhat moralistic term for alcoholism, suggesting principally a failure of self-control

intoximeter * an uncommon synonym for breathalyzer

J

jakelegged * paralyzed as a consequence of drinking 'jake', an old patent tonic containing 85% medicinal alcohol

jecorary * pertaining to the liver

K

katzenjammer * a thorough-going hangover headache

Korsakoff's psychosis * long-term memory loss and brain damage through protein deficiency secondary to hard-core alcoholism

THE DRINKTIONARY

L

Laënnec's syndrome * cirrhosis of the liver, commonly with alcohol-related aetiology

liferadl * liver disease, in Old English

liverishness * the condition of having a diseased or damaged liver

lurgies * colloquially, the hangover blues

M

mania crapulosa * a mania for intoxicating drink

mania temulentia * mania caused by intoxicating drink

maniportia * Maryland vernacular for the DTs; from 'mania a potu' – madness from drinking

mawmsey * brain-fogged and lethargic through over-imbibing the night before

metadoxine * a drug acting to accelerate the clearance of alcohol from the bloodstream

methexiphrenesis * the terminal stage of acute alcoholism

methobiostatics * research into the constitutional effects of alcoholic excess

methogastrosis * marked digestive disturbance due to heavy drinking

methylepsia * a gripping, clinical compulsion to drink

methysis * a now-abandoned synonym for alcoholism

methyspomania * a morbid desire for alcohol

Milwaukee goitre * a beer-belly – after the self-proclaimed 'beer capital of the world'

mokus * depressed in drink; a term formerly used in AA circles for alcoholic self-loathing and the mental confusion experienced as one dries out

N

naltrexone * a medication efficacious in reducing dependence on drink

narcomania * insanity from the abuse of narcotics or alcohol

O

oenilism * a form of alcoholism caused by the immoderate consumption of wine

oinomania * alcohol craving and dependency

ork-orks * informally, delirium tremens

ornithine * a variant amino acid produced by the liver, used to treat cirrhosis

P

paradipsia * a perverted appetite for drink bearing no relation to any reasonable physiological or psychological requirements

penny-pots * pimples or liver spots on the face betraying a hardened drinker

philoenia * a pathological addiction to wine or strong drink

polyalcoholism * the coterminous abuse of multiple alcoholic beverages

port-complexioned * flushed or florid through years of devoted wine drinking

posiomania * long-term alcohol abuse

potative * addicted to intoxicating beverages

potomania * a syndrome of serious medical impairments arising from the gross consumption of beer, otherwise known as 'beer drinker's hyponatraemia'

pototromoparanoia * delirium tremens in extremis

pseudotabes alcoholica * the loss of motor coordination owing to habitual drunkenness

pyrithioxine * a drug feasibly effective as a hangover cure if taken in large doses

Q

quart-mania * colloquially, delirium tremens or the DTs

S

samidorphan * a medication under investigation for its potential efficacy in the management of alcohol dependency

stale-drunk * hungover

swollenhead * a hangover

T

tremor potatorum * delirium tremens

tyramine * a compound found in robust red wines such as Chianti, once blamed for causing headaches and hangovers

U

unsober * routinely indisposed through addiction to drink

V

veisalgia * a hangover, in clinical parlance

vinnecky-vasky * nursing a hangover

vinose * addicted to wine

W

wamble-cropped * suffering an upset stomach due to heavy drinking

whisky-tacket * a blemish emblematic of overindulgence in spirituous liquors

wine-ensanguined * rosy or ruddy of face from the copious consumption of wine

Z

zooscopic * seeing the proverbial 'pink elephants' through drinking to excess

10
UPON SOBER REFLECTION
– TEMPERANCE & TEETOTALISM –

A

abstainer * a nondrinker or teetotaller

abstemiousness * disciplined avoidance of strong drink

alcoholophobia * fear of the effects or consequences of inebriation

amphibious * neither 'wet' nor 'dry', as twenties America where the production and consumption of alcohol remained widespread despite officially being outlawed

antiliquor * opposing or serving to frustrate the consumption of alcoholic beverages

aquabib * one who shuns alcohol, in mocking reference to a 'water drinker'

B

bluenose * a blue-ribbonite or teetotal puritan

blue-ribbonism * militant evangelical teetotalism

C

cagg * to take a solemn vow to refrain from liquor for a designated period of time, typically one month

D

dipsomanophobia * aversion to drink from fear of addiction to its intoxicating properties and consequentially becoming an alcoholic derelict

dryathlon * a voluntary extended period of abstinence from alcohol, regarded as an ordeal of endurance

F

fastidium potus * profound loathing for intoxicating liquor

flincher * one averse to and who avoids alcohol

G

Good Templardom * the freemasonry of crusading abstainers

H

hydropote * an abstemious type; one who partakes of nothing stronger than water

hydropotic * temperate or teetotal

J

Janopause * reparative or resolutional abstention from alcohol following the excesses of the New Year's celebrations

jook-the-bottle * an Ulsterman who has renounced alcohol

L

lewis cornaro * an advocate of temperance as a means to a long and healthy life

M

methyphobia * an encompassing fear of alcohol, including proximity to persons under its influence

moderationist * a campaigner for more responsible drinking

N

neoprohibitionism * the belief that alcohol consumption should be controlled and drinking culture reformed through tough social and legislative action

nephalism * a synonym for teetotalism

O

oenophobist * one who possesses a strong dislike of or aversion to wine

P

phobodipsia * fear of acquiring a thirst for strong drink

pioneer * one who has taken the pledge to desist thereafter from alcohol

potophobia * fear of drinking intoxicating beverages, intentionally or in error

prohibition * a ban on the production, distribution, sale and consumption of alcohol

pussyfootism * opposition to the consumption of intoxicating liquor

R

Rechabitism * abstention from alcohol on scriptural grounds

rumhound * an agent of the state charged with upholding the writ of prohibition

S

soberize * to sober up

sobriety * a condition free from alcoholic intoxication

T

teakettle purger * one who strictly shuns inebriating drink

teetalitarian * a Joycean coinage deriding joyless and authoritarian prohibitionist impulses and policies

teetotaciously * in a thoroughly abstemious and morally upright manner

teetotalism * absolute renunciation of and abstention from potent beverages

teetotalized * converted to teetotalism

teetotalleress * a female who desists from drinking

temperance * abstention from the consumption of intoxicating drink

U

unebriate * not intoxicated

unliquored * dry; sober

V

Volsteadism * the American historical experience of prohibition, after Andrew J Volstead who sponsored the antiliquor act passed in 1919 which bore his name

W

Washingtonian * a member of a former friendly society devoted to the pursuit of a dry society

wowserism * god-fearing or otherwise fanatical opposition to the demon drink

SELECT BIBLIOGRAPHY & WEBLIOGRAPHY

Boulton, Chris. *Encyclopaedia of Brewing*. (Oxford: John Wiley & Sons, 2013)
Dickson, Paul. *Intoxerated: The Definitive Drinker's Dictionary*. (NY: Melville House Publishing, 2012)
Dictionary of the Scots Language. <http://www.dsl.ac.uk/>
English Dialect Dictionary. <http://eddonline-proj.uibk.ac.at/edd/index.jsp>
English Vocabulary Word Directory. <http://www.wordinfo.info/words/index/info/>
Farmer, John S & Henley, WE. *A Dictionary of Slang & Colloquial English*. (London: George Routledge & Sons, 1921)
Gately, Iain. *Drink: A Cultural History of Alcohol*. (NY: Gotham Books, 2008)
Green, Jonathon. *The Cassell Dictionary of Slang*. (London: Cassell, 1998)
Historical Thesaurus of English. <http://historicalthesaurus.arts.gla.ac.uk/>
Hornsey, Ian S. *A History of Beer & Brewing*. (Cambridge: Royal Society of Chemistry, 2003)
Martin, Scott C (ed). *The SAGE Encyclopedia of Alcohol: Social, Cultural, & Historical Perspectives* (Los Angeles: SAGE Publications, 2015)
Oliver, Garrett (ed). *The Oxford Companion to Beer*. (NY: OUP, 2011)
Oxford English Dictionary. <http://www.oed.com/>
Rabin, Dan & Forget, Carl. *The Dictionary of Beer & Brewing*. (Chicago, Fitzroy Dearborn Publishers, 1998)
Robinson, Jancis (ed). *The Oxford Companion to Wine*. (OUP, 1994)
Rogers, Adam. *Proof: The Science of Booze*. (NY: Houghton Mifflin Harcourt, 2014)
Shipley, Joseph T. *Dictionary of Early English*. (Paterson, NJ: Littlefield, Adams & Co, 1963)
Simon, André L. *A Dictionary of Wines, Spirits & Liqueurs*. (London: Herbert Jenkins, 1958)
Thesaurus of Old English. <http://libra.englang.arts.gla.ac.uk/oethesaurus/>
Walton, Stuart & Glover, Brian. *The Ultimate Encyclopedia of Wine, Beer, Spirits & Liqueurs*. (London: Hermes House, 2006)
Wikipedia. <https://en.wikipedia.org/wiki/Portal:Drink>

AN A–Z OF ENTRIES

A

Abraham grains * abroach * absintheur * absinthiana * absinthism * absinthites * abs-lushery * abstainer * abstemiousness * acamprosate * acataposis * acerglyn * acetabulum * acetaldehyde * acetobacter * acidulation * acraipala * acratism * adhumulone * adipson * adipsy * Admiral of the Narrow Seas * adrench * aeppelwin * aeration * agrafe * alabandical * alabazam * alappanu * alcogene * alcohol * alcohol absolutum * alcohol amnestic syndrome * alcohol dilutum * alcohol ethylicum * alcohol methylicum * alcoholature * alcoholdyscrasia * alcoholic cardiomyopathy * alcoholic hallucinosis * alcoholic steatohepatitis * alcoholicity * alcoholiday * alcoholism * alcoholist * alcoholizate * alcoholization * alcoholizer * alcohology * alcoholomania * alcoholophilia * alcoholophobia * alcoholosis * alcoholpseudoparalysis * alcoholuria * alcoometer * alcopop * alcovinometer * Alderman Lushington * aleboly * aleconner * alecy * ale-drapery * alegar * ale-knight * ale-passion * ale-score * Alicant * alkermes * alleviator * allicholy * allslops * almacenista * alpha alcoholic * altogethery * amethysum * ammoniacal * ampelideous * ampelography * ampelopsin * amphibious * amphora * ampulla * anaconda * anacreontic * angels' share * anker * antabuse * ante-meridian * anthine * anthocyanins * anthracnose * anti-fogmatic * anti-guggler * antihepatotoxicity * antiliquor * antiposia * antizymotic * antlia gastrica * aperitif * apoplexy * apostles * appale * appassimento * appellation * applejack * apple-palsy * apron-washings * aqua composita * aqua mirabilis * aquabib * aquavit * aqua-vitae * arbiter bibendi * archbishop * archdeacon * archilaugh * ardaunt * Argentarium * argol * aristippus * aristotle * ars cervesaria * artesian * artilleryman * assemblage * astringent * Athole brose * atom-bombo * attemperator * attenuation * Aurum potabile * auto-brewery syndrome * autolytic * autovinification * awerdenty

B

bacchanalia * bacchanalize * bacchant * bacchation * Bacchi plenus * Bacchus * Badminton cup * baijiu * balderdash * balductum * balthazar * bappir * baptized * barefooted * barfly * barleybree * barleycap * barleyhood * barley-island * barm * barm-feast * barmigen * baron * barrelage * barrel-fever * barrelhouse * barrique * bastard * bâtonnage * beerage * beer-bibber * beer-bombard * beer-brussen * beer-buzzer * beerflation * beerhood * beerienteering * beerified * beer-jerker * beer-jugger * beer-monger * beerness * beernoculars * beerocracy * beersicle * beerstone * beeswinged * befuddlement * Belgian lace * beliquor * bellarmine * bene-bowse * benjamin * bentonite * beorsele * berkemeyer * besotted * bethphany * betipple * bever * beverage * beverageware * bevvy omee * bezzler * bezzling * bibacious * bibamus papaliter! * bibation * bibativeness * bibbership * bibbery * biberage * biberon * Bibesia * bibesy * bibibles * bibitory * bibosity * bibster * bibulant * bibulate * bibulosity * bibulous * bidon * biergarten * bierstiefel * bierzwang * bilgewater * bimbo * bingo * bingo-mort * birling * Bismarck * bistrot * blastophthoria * blind tiger * blindo * blitzkrieged * blouperd * blow-bowl * bluenose * blue-ribbonism * bluestone * bochetomel * bocksbeutel * bodega * Bohemian bungery * boilermaker * boisson-totem * bombard * bonally * boniface * bootlegging * boozefest * boozeroo * boozician * boozify * boozorium * borachio * boskiness * botanicals * bothan * botryosphaeria * botrytized * bottle-crony * bottle-swagger * bottled lightning * bottlery * bottomer * bouquet * bourbonization * bourgeois * bouza * bowsered * brachetour * braga-beaker * braggot * Brahms & Liszt * brandified * brandy galaxy * brandy-cleek * brandy-shunter * brandy-spinner * brannigan * brasserie * breathalyzer * brendice * brettanomyces * brewage * breweriana * brewer's asthma * brewership * brewhaha * brewhouse * brewicide * brewpub * brewster * brewster session * brilliancy * brimmer * brimmered * brindize * British burgundy * broaching * bromelains * Bromian * bromsulphthalein

* brother bung * brouillis * Brummagem wine * bruthen-lead * brutify'd * bucellas * budge kain * bumbaste * bumbo * bumclink * bumper * bunghole * burtonization * bush champagne * butlerage * butt * buttery * buttling * buvable * buvette * bybbe

C

caback * cagg * calandria * calcatory * calibogus * calyx-crater * campaniled * canette * canteen medal * cantharus * cantina * cantling * capernoity * capsicumel * capsuling * carafe * carbo-load * carboy * caritas * caroenum * carousal * cask-conditioned * casse * catacomb * caudalie * caudle * caulker * cellaragium * cellaret * cellarist * cellarmanship * cellar-physic * cépage * cerevisaphile * cerevisious * cerevisium duplex * cervesarius * cervisia * chalice * Chambertin * chambré * Champagne Charley * champagnish * chaptalization * Chardonnization * Charenton omnibus * charmat * chasse-café * chateau collapse-o * chateaued * chemesthesis * chemically inconvenienced * cherry-merry * cherubimical * chevalier * chhaang * chicha * chillproof * chirruper * chloroanisoles * chloroformed * chlorophenolic * chopin * chopine * choppin * chug-a-lug! * chunder bunny * churchkey * cider-country * ciderist * ciderkin * cider-master * ciderspace * cidery * cinchonism * circumcellion * cirrhogenous * cirrhosis * citroned * clamberskull * clank-napper * claret-cunner * clareteer * clary * classico * clavelin * clear-crystal * clovelike * clurichaun * co-alcoholic * cobbler * cochineal * cockers-p * cocktail * cocktailed * cocktailian * cogueful * cohobation * columbered * comboozelated * comet-hock * comical farce * Commanderia * complantation * complexity * compotationship * compotator * comus * conditum paradoxum * congelation * congeners * congius * connywobble * consolation * constitutional * continentality * cool-nantz * coolship * cooper * cooperage * copita * copus * copyholder * cordial * cordialine * cordialize * corkage * corkedness * Cornelius keg * corporation

THE DRINKTIONARY

cocktail * corpse-reviver * cosmopolitan * cosmos * costrel * cottabus * cranberry-eye * crapula * crapulency * crapulental * crapulosity * cratur * crawsick * crémant * crianza * croze * crusta * cryoextraction * cryptogamic * cultivar * cup-conqueror * cupshodden * cupstantial * curjute * curwhibbles * cuvaison * cuvée * cuvier * cyathus * cyclone * cymaise

D

daffier * daktulosphaira * damask * damper * Darwin stubby * dealcoholization * debacchate * debilitate * decantation * decanter * decks-awash * deculming * defrutum * degrees Brix * degrees Gay-Lussac * degrees Plato * dehorn * dehorner * delestage * delibate * delicatessen * delirium ebriosorum * delphine * demiard * demijohn * demi-muid * demoiselle * denatonium benzoate * denaturation * deoch-an-doris * dephlegmator * detoxification * diapente * diddle-cove * digester * dihydromyricetin * dingbatisis * dionysiac * dipsomaniac * dipsomaniacal * dipsomanophobia * dipsopathy * dipsorexia * discask * disgorgement * disintoxication * dispense * dispirited * distempering * distillage * distillation * distillatory * distilleress * distillery * distilment * disulfiram * ditchwateriness * dobbin * doble-doble * dolium * domaine * doppelbock * doppelstück * dopskal * dosage * doundrins * dragon's milk * dramming * drammist * dram-shop * draught * drayman * drenchus * driffling * drillopota * drinkage * drinkative * drinkdom * drink-drowned * drinkeress * drinkery * drink-hail * drinking-do * drinkitite * drink-silver * drinkware * drinkworthy * drinkypoo * dronklap * drouthy * druncenscipe * drunkalog * drunkardize * drunkelewness * drunkensome * drunkify * drunkometer * drunkorexia * drunkship * dryathlon * dryhopping * drynchorn * dubbel * Dutch doggery * dwale * dwile flonking * dyshepatia * dyskataposis

E

eau-de-vie * ebibe * ebriection * ebrietating * ebriety * ebrilagnia * ebriosity * ebulum * effervescence * elixir * emperor * empress * encépagement * enfant-Jésus * enfumed * enoteca * envined * epotation * epsilon alcoholic * Est! Est!! Est!!! * estaminet * estery * estufagem * ethanol * ethanolic * ethenol * evaporative perstraction * ewery * excoriose * expansive * exuberant * eyebright

F

family-disturbance * farintosh * faro * fastidium potus * Father-Whoresonne * favourite vice * fearnought * febrifuge * fecula * fermentation * fermentologist * fermentology * festbier * fetal alcohol syndrome * feuillet * fiasco * fillette * finesse * firewater * firkin * fix bayonets * fizzical culturalist * flagon * flagonal * flagonet * flatch-kennurd * flincher * flor * floradora * flosculous * flustrated * flute * fobbing * fogmatic * fogram * foozlified * fordrunken * foreshots * formication * fortification * fou * foulage * fountain * fourquette * foxing * fox-whelp * Frankenwine * freeholder * French 75 * fretting * friabilimeter * frizzle * frommeling * frontloading * fudder * fuddlecap * fumarium * fumosity * fustage * fustian

G

galactozyme * galliack * gallization * gallon-distemper * galopin * gambarius * gambrinous * Gambrinus * gamma alcoholism * Ganymedean * garagiste * gargle * gargle-factory * gargolette * gasthaus * gastric lavage * gastropub * gatter * gauntress * gebeorscipe * genevaed * gentilize * geosmin * geropiga * gibberellins * giggle-water * gilravage * ginnified *

THE DRINKTIONARY

ginnums * gin-palace * gintellectual * giracleur * giraffe * glassware * glögg * glowsing * gluconobacter * gluggable * glutathione * goblet * gobleter * godalier * godisgood * goliath * gönc * Good Templardom * goth * governo * grapelage * grape-monger * grapeshot * grayhead * groatable * grog * grog-blossom * groggified * growler * guardevine * gueuzier * gulch-cup * gusano * gustator cerevisiae * guttle * guzzery * guzzle-guts * gyle * gyllot * gyropalette

H

haberdasher * habillage * hailstorm * halbfüder * halbtrocken * hanap * hanepoot * hatchetation * haustor * hausture * heartsease * heebie-jeebies * heeltap * hellbroth * helvine * hemina * hepatonecrosis * hepatopathy * hepatoprotective * hepatotoxic * herbaceous * hermitage * heuriger * hicksius doxius * hippocras * hirculation * hobbernobbering * hockamore * hocus * hogshead * hokonui * homerkin * homo imbibens * hoochinoo * hophead * hopine * hoppenbier * horizontal * hostelaphily * hovenia * howff * howling Modoc * huffcap * hukster * humming October * humpty-dumpty * humulus lupulus * hydromel * hydrometer * hydropote * hydropotic * hyperalcoholaemia * hyperposia

I

icterohepatitis * ikkinomi * imbiber * imbibition * imp of the spigot * imperial * impixlocated * impotant * impote * impotentia alcoholica * inabstinent * incognitibus * incrocio * indrunken * inebriacy * inebriate * inebriation * inebriism * inebrious * ingenio * ingestar * inky-pinky * innholder * insobriety * intemperancy * intemperant * inter pocula * intoxicant * intoxicated *

PAUL CONVERY

intoxicator * intoximeter * invertebrated * invigorator * invination * ipsydinxy * irp * irrigate * ishkimmisk * ivresse * ivy-garland * izakaya

J

jackpot * Jacobite * Jagerette * jakelegged * Janopause * jarman * jecorary * jeroboam * jerrawicke * jigger * jiggerstuff * jingle * jingle-box * John Barleycorn * jointist * jollify * jollop * jolly-boys * jook-the-bottle * jorum * joven * joy-juice * jubbe * jubilated * jug-bitten * juggins-hunting * jungbukett

K

kaniker * kapelion * kastenlauf * katzenjammer * kegerator * kegging * kelty mends * kerotakis * khamriyya * kiddleywink * kieselguhr * kilderkin * kill-devil * kill-priest * kilning * kimnel * klosterbräu * knight of the spigot * komastic * korma * Korsakoff's psychosis * kovsh * krasis * krateriskos * krausening * kurabito * kvass * kylix

L

labeorphilist * Lacrima Christi * Laënnec's syndrome * lagale * lagar * lagenarious * lagering * lagerphone * lambic * lancepresado * langerated * lantify * lautermash * lavative * lazy ballerina * leaguer * lechayim! * lembic * lewis cornaro * libament * libation * libationer * libatory * Liebfraumilch * liferadl * lightstruck * limonadier * Lintner * liqueur * liquid lunch * liquidation * liquor * liquordom * liquorhead * liquorishness * liquorist * liquoroso * liquor-seasoned * liverishness * locapour * locomotive * locus

THE DRINKTIONARY

* loll-shraub * London particular * longbeard * longwhiskey * lora * lotion * louching * loveage * Lovibond * lubricated * lubrication * lunatic broth * lunel * lupomaniac * lupuline * lupulite * lurgies * lurrep * lushery * lushings * lushwell * lust-house * lustick * Lyaeus * lymphate

M

maceration * macro-oxygenation * Madame Geneva * maderize * madza-beargered * magnum * magnum bonum * mahogany * Maitrank * mallemaroking * malmsey * malt-bree * malternative * maltings * malt-inspired * malt-surrogate * malty-cove * mandragora * mania crapulosa * mania temulentia * maniportia * manipulant * marc * marinated * Martin-drunk * masculine * mash-tub * masseria * master of the wardrobe * matrimony * maudlinize * mavrodaphne * mawmsey * maximus * max-ken * mazzard * meadery * meadist * meadophily * mealer * mealtgesceot * meduburg * meduwong * megasphaera * melchior * melchizedek * melicrate * mercaptans * meregoutte * merissa * meritage * merry-go-down * merulator * metadoxine * methanol * metheglin * methexiphrenesis * metho * methobiostatics * méthode champenoise * methodistconated * methogastrosis * methuselah * methylated spirits * methylepsia * methyphobia * methysis * methyspomania * methystic * mezcal * microbrewery * microbullage * microchâteau * microdistillery * microvinification * middy * millerandage * millésime * Milwaukee goitre * minerality * miniature * Missae de Potatoribus * mistelle * mixologist * mocktail * moderationist * modicum * moelleux * mokus * molecular mixology * monocépage * monongahela * monopole * monovarietal * monteith * montejus * moonshiner * morat * morning's draughtman * Morocco * moroculous * mortallious * mother-in-law * mountflascon * mousseline * mousseux * moustille * mouthfeel * mouthwash * muckibus * mugroom * muller * mulsum * multibibe *

multum * mulvathered * mumbo-jum * muscadoodle * muscateer * muselet * mustulent * mutchkin * mutism * muzzler * muzzling * mycoderma vini * myrcene * myrtite

N

naggin * naltrexone * nanobrewery * napper tandy * narcomania * narcomaniac * nazy * nebuchadnezzar * négociant * negus * neknominate * neoprohibitionism * neo-speakeasy * nephalism * nestoposia * ney-beer * nickum * nightcap * nihonshu * nimptopsical * Ninkasi * nip joint * nipperkin * nippitatum * nitrokeg * nitro-muddling * nittiness * nobbler * noggin * non-alcoholic beverage * non-beverage alcohol * nonic * noonshine * Norfolk-nog * nor'-wester * norwicher * nouveau * nux-vomicize

O

oaking * oast-house * o-be-joyfuller * obesumbacterium * obfusticated * ochorboc * octave * oeil-de-perdrix * oenanthic * oenilism * oenochemistry * oenochoe * oenocyanin * oenogen * oenolagnia * oenology * oenomancy * oenomaniac * oenomel * oenophil * oenophily * oenophlygia * oenophobist * oenophorum * oenotourism * Oenotria * off-licensee * ogogoro * oidium * oil of barley * oinomania * oinopoetic * Oktoberfest * Old Pharaoh * oligophorous * oloroso * ombibulus * omnes * omnibibulous * omnipotans * omphacomel * Opimian * optic * opticity * opulent * ordinary * organolepsis * ork-orks * ornithine * ouzeria * overdecking * overhopped * overproof * oxhoft * oxidative * oxycrocium

THE DRINKTIONARY

P

palatic * palintoshed * pampination * pantagruelist * panther-piss * paradipsia * pariah-arrack * paroinia * parti-gyle * passerillage * passglas * passito * patent-digester * patera * paxarette * peat-reek * peloothered * pelure d'oignon * penitentiary highball * penny-pots * penny-wheep * pepst * periodics * perlant * perpendicular drinking * perpotation * persicot * peterman * Peter-see-me * pétillance * petiotization * pevakh * phellem * philanthropissed * philharmonic * philistine * philoenia * philopotes * phlegm cutter * phobodipsia * phosphotage * Phrygian grog * phuza-cabin * phylloxerated * piccolo * pigeage * piggin * pigtail * Pillahuana * pilsener * Pimlico * pinard * pincern * pint-stoup * pioneer * pipe-merry * pipot * piquette * piriwhit * pirliewink * pisco * pißwasser * pitcherful * pitcher-meat * pitcher-praise * pivophilia * pixilated * Plimsole line * plinkity-plonk * plonko * pocill * pocillation * pocket pistol * poculary * poculation * poculent * poculum * pokal * polyalcoholism * polydipsia * polyphorous * polypin * polyposist * polyvinylpolypyrrolidone * pomace * pommage * pomperkin * pongellorum * pontacq * popinal * popination * popinjay * popskull * porrón * port-complexioned * porterhouse * posadaship * posca * posiomania * posset * post-meridian * potability * potation * potationist * potative * potatories * potatory * potboydom * pot-companioning * poteen * potence * pot-goddardine * pot-housey * potisuge * potiuncle * potomania * potomaniac * potophobia * potorious * pototromoparanoia * potpanion * pot-parliament * pot-proof-armour * pot-punishment * potsmitten * pottical * pottle-bottle * potulent * potvaliantry * pot-vertigo * pot-walloper * pourboire * pousse-café * poverty * powsoddy * Pramnian * precocious * prefillossero * preimbibe * prelibation * premox * pressourhouse * Priapus vitreus * prima melior * primeur * primitive * prisage * proface! * prohibition * propination * propinatrix * propine * propoma * propriétaire * Province of Bacchus * pruss * pseudodipsomania * pseudoperonospora

PAUL CONVERY

* pseudotabes alcoholica * psykter * pubco * publicanism * puckery * pug-drink * puggle-pawnee * pulqueria * puncheon * punchery * punch-house * punchifier * punt * pupitre * purchase * purl-boat * purling * purl-royal * purple para * pussyfoot * pussyfootism * puttonyos * pyment * pyrazines * pyrithioxine

Q

quadrantal * quadrimium * quadrupel * quaffable * quafftide * quaich * qualifier * qualitätswein * qually * quantum * quare stuff (the) * quartern * quartern o'finger * quart-mania * quaught * Queen of Scotch * queer belch * queer-bluffer * queer-nantz * quinquina * quinta * quintessence * qvevri

R

racemation * rambooze * ramsquaddled * rancio * raspays * ratafia * rathskeller * Rechabitism * récoltant * rectification * red-lattice * reductionist * refreshment * rehoboam * Reinheitsgebot * remontage * remuage * reposer * resveratrol * reswill * reticent * retro-olfaction * revelation * reverent * Rhenish * rhodomel * rhyton * rickhouse * rinse-pitcher * ripasso * River Ouse * rivo! * roberdavy * Rodney * rompney * rookus-juice * rorty * rosasolis * rosiner * rotofermenter * rotovap * rotundone * rouzy-bouzy * Royal Usquebaugh * rubbity-dub * Rum Row * rumbowling * rumbullion * rumbustion * rumfustian * rumhound * rummager * rummarian * rummer * rummery * rum-running * rundlet

S

sabrage * Saccharomyces bayanus * Saccharomyces cerevisiae * Saccharomyces pastorianus * sack-butt * sack-guzzler * sack-sopt * sackwah * sagittary * sagwire * sakazuki * sakery * sallivocus * salmanazar * saloon smasher * samidorphan * samogon * sampson * samshoo * sangaree * Saprian * sarcophagus * sauce-hound * savoir boire * scheelization * schnappsteufeln * schooner * sconcing * Scotch by absorption * scotchem * Scotchification * scuddiness * scuppernong * scurvygrass-ale * scuttered * seau * seidel * semibousy * semisecco * Septembral juice * sercial * serpentary * sester * sève * sextary * Shaftesbury * shakerful * shakparo * shamrock * shandygaff * shebang * shebeen queen * shedista * shellacked * shenkbeer * shenker * sherrified * sherris-sack * shetland * shickerhood * shoful * shooper * shot-clog * shot-flagon * shot-shark * shuffler * shypoo * sicer * Silenus * silex * Sillery * silver-fizz * Simon pure * simpkin * simpulum * singleton * singlings * sipple * Sir Cloudesley * sirocco * siwash * sixteens * skeachen * skew-whiff * skimmisher * skinful * skinking-pot * skoaling * skylight * skyphos * sky-wannocking * slainte! * slinger * slobber * slop-beg * slopping-up * sloshery * sluicery * sly-grogster * smahan * smirking * snapdragon * snapsvisa * snifter * snoozamorooed * snorkel * snowbroth * snuggery * soberize * sobriety * sobriety-deprived * solera * solomon * solventy * somalamma * sommelier * sooming * sorbillate * sorbition * sosselled * sot's-hof * sottishness * sora * sorbicle * sotol * sottefer * soutirage * sou'-wester * sovereign * soyeux * sparging * spätlese * speakeasy * spencer * spewterer * spicket-wench * spifflicated * spigot * spiritualized * spirituosity * spiritus frumenti * spiritus pyroxylicus * spiritus rectificatus * spiritus vini gallici * spodiodi * sponage * spoofilated * sprightful * spritzer * spritzig * spumante * spunkie * squareface * squeaker * squeans * squencher * squire of the gimlet * St Arnoldus * St Bibiana * St Lubbock * St Martin * St Vincent Saragossa * stagma * stalagma * stale-drunk * staling * stalkiness * steelyard * steinkrug * stellatour * stelvin

* stemware * stengah * stepony * stewed Quaker * stiefeltrinken * stillatitious * stillified * stillion * stillroom * stimulants * stingo * stinkibus * stinko paralytico * stirrup-cup * stocious * stonkering * stratosphere * stravecchio * strip-me-naked * strongers * strunt * stumblebum * stumming * stuykmanden * Stygian liquor * submarino * suck-casa * suckerdom * suction * suds factory * sulphurated * summer-barmed * sundowner * superbibe * supernacular * supernaculum * Super-Tuscans * su-pouch * supping-stuff * surfeit waters * Surrentine * süssreserve * svagdricka * swamper * swankey * swatan * swattle * swigsby * swillery * swilliking * swillocks * swinking * swipington * swish-swash * switchel * swizzlement * swizzler * swizzle-stick * swollenhead * symbelwlonc * symposiarch * symposiast * symposium * synthehol * Syracuse

T

tabernarious * tafelwein * taggeen * tallboy * tanglefooted * tankard * tankard-yeoman * tantalus * tanzemann * taplash * tappit-hen * tapstership * tapstry * tarantula-juice * tartrates * tastevin * tavern-discourse * taverner * taverning * tavernize * tavernry * tea-canister * teakettle purger * tears of the tankard * teetalitarian * teetotaciously * teetotalism * teetotalized * teetotalleress * teetotum * tegestologist * teinturier * temperance * temperer * temulency * temulentive * terroir * tersail * tertian * thermopolite * thermopolium * thermopoly * thermopot * thermopotis * thermovinification * thirdendeal * thirst-aid station * thirstington * three-heads * thujone * tickle-brain * tight as Andronicus * tiltings * timber-doodle * timothy * tincture * Tipperary * tipplage * tipple square * tippler * tippling * tipsification * tipsificator * tirage * tired & emotional * Tirosh * tiswin * titanic * titubancy * titubant * toddyize * tokkori * tolsester * Tom-and-Jerry * Tom-and-Jerryism * tonneau * toothful * toperdom * toperism * torcula * torp * torrification * tosspotlike * tosticated * tovarich * toxified * transparency * transversage * trantery * Trappist * treble

X * tregnum * tremor potatorum * trestarig * tribromoanisole * triental * trillil * trimmings * tripel * trockenbeerenauslese * trusty Trojan * tsipouro * tub * tulip * tumbler * tumbrel * tunc * tunhoof * tunnery * turbidity * turbinaceous * turps-nudger * twankay * twibrowen * twoops * tyg * typicity * tyramine

U

ullage * unalcoholized * unctuous * uncuted * undercarbonated * under-skinner * unebriate * uninebriating * uni-tank * unliquored * unsober * unstoppered * unullaged * uphale * upsy Dutch * upsy English * urceolus * Urquell * uscova * utepils * uting * uviferous

V

valincher * vappa * varietal * varnished * vatful * vatting * vegetal * veisalgia * vendonging * venenciador * veraison * vermouth * versor * vertical * vespitro * Vice-Admiral of the Narrow Seas * viertel * vigneron * vignette * vin d'honneur * vinaceous * vinacre * vinager * vinarious * vinasse * vindemiatory * vindemiatrix * vinegarist * vine-garth * vine-husbandry * vineyardist * vinic * viniculture * viniferous * vinification * vinimatic * vinipote * vinitorian * vinnecky-vasky * vino maestro * vinolence * vinologist * vinomadefied * vinometry * vinose * vinosity * vintage * vintager * vintnephilist * vintnery * vintry * vinum absinthiatum * vinum album * vinum campanum * vinum portense * vinum rubrum * vinum theologium * vinum xericum * virgin wine * visney * vitamin XXX * viticetum * viticide * viticulturalist * viticulture * vitigineous * Vitis labrusca * Vitis vinifera * vodkatini * volatile * Volsteadism * von-blinked * vulcanized

W

wallop * wamble-cropped * wampo * warnage * Washingtonian * wassailry * water bewitched * water intoxication * waterberry * waterlogged * waterloo * waughting * wazzocked * weeper * Weihenstephan * whemmel * whetter * whippincrust * whirlpooling * whiskey priest * whiskified * whiskin * whiskybae * whisky-fair * whiskyish * whisky-skin * whisky-tacket * whistle-belly-vengeance * whistling-shop * whitewash * whoopensocker * widget * wiederkom * willybecher * winbrytta * wineathlon * wineberg * wine-ensanguined * wineland * winemanship * winery * wineskin * wine-snobbery * winespeak * wingemang * winston * wintrog * witblitz * wobble-shop * wodky * wort * wowserism * wusa

X, Y, Z

xanthohumol * Ximenes * yack-yack bourbon * yal-yottler * Yankee particular * yard of ale * ydrunken * yeast-bitten * yeovale * yile-tun * yill * yilling * ysell * Yukon mickey * yvronke * zapoy * zarab * zasmidium * zawker * zegedine * zentner * zeoscope * zibeeb * zigzag * zinc * zinfandel * zooscopic * zopy * zubrowka * zuckerpilz * zumology * zwaartbier * zymase * zymolysis * zymomonas * zymoscope * zymosimetry * zymotechnics * zymotechnology * zymurgist * zymurgy * zythepsary * zythophile * zythum

THE DRINKTIONARY

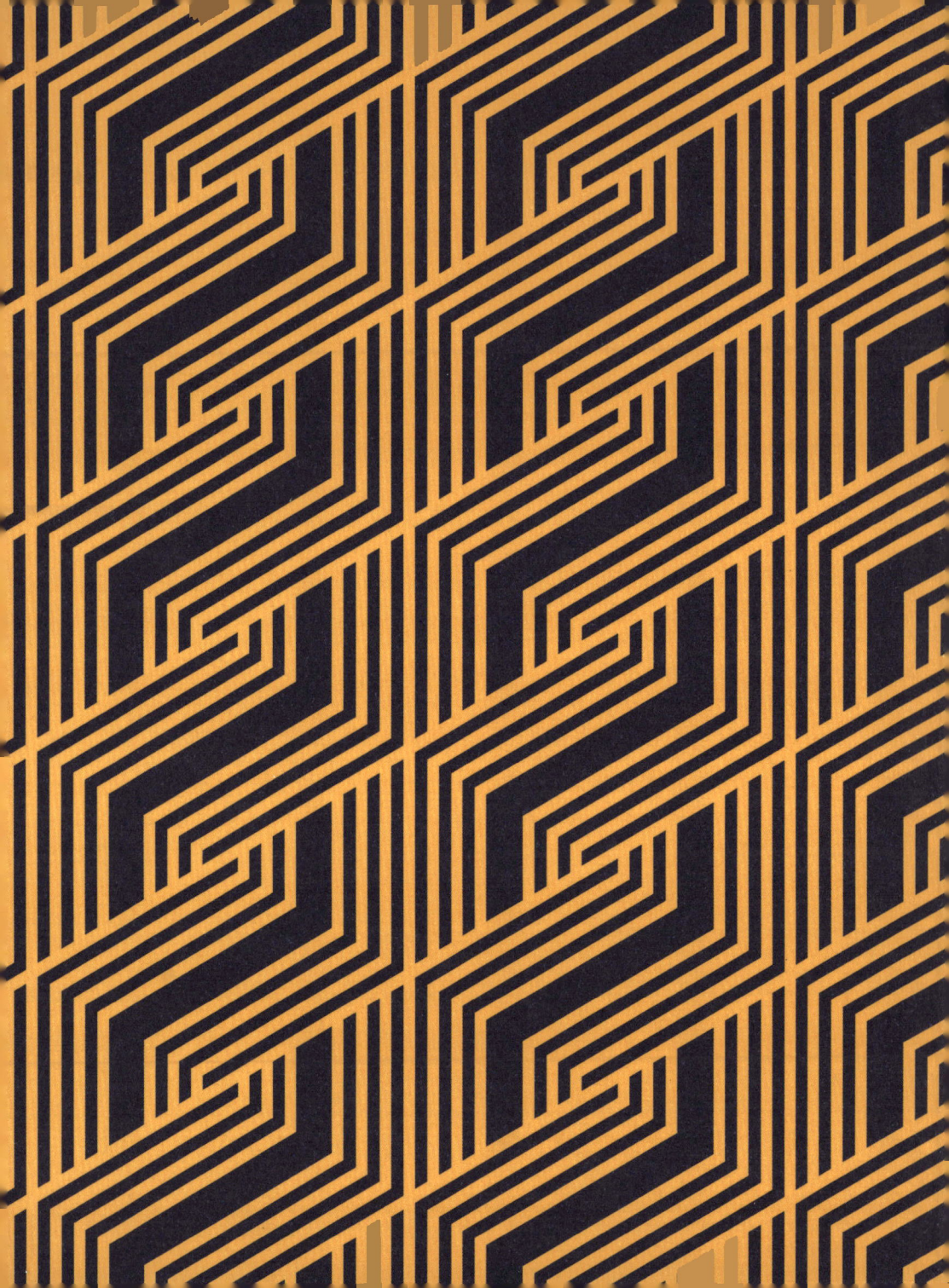